SUCCESSFUL SELLING

Learn how.

Graeme Smith

PUBLISHED ON AMAZON.com
by
LABYRINTH BOOKS

DEDICATION:

This book is dedicated to my family.

Hele-ly (Ly).
       my wife:

Ingrid.
       our daughter:

Marie.
       my former wife:

Fiona, Natalie and Michael
       our children:

Georgie
       Michael's wife:

Pearl, Kiki and Martha.
       their children:

They have had to put up with me for many years and I thank them for that.
I hope this book gives them an insight into what has occupied me.
All have done worthwhile and interesting things in the absence of my help.
I congratulate them for their achievements.

HOW TO USE THIS BOOK.

First think - then do.
Usually people don't think through things to the level they need to.
Because of that, they have projects instead of tasks on their "to do" list.
That leads to procrastination as it hasn't been broken down to a task level.

So go through your book once to understand it.
Go through it again.

Then start at the idea you would like to implement first.
Make notes of the steps you will need to take and the resources required.
Use these notes to create a step by step system for implementing the guide.
Often you will not refer to the original, once you've created **YOUR** system.

The first question to ask and answer is "Why is this being done?"
How does this align with where you want to get to?
What are the strategic implications of doing this?
Does this fit with getting to your goal in the shortest and fastest time?
What would it be like if it were totally successful?
Define it - what is success for this project and how will you know?

Now brainstorm all the tasks that are involved in your project.
It's important not to go linear too fast with this.
By linear, I mean step one, step two, step three, and step four.
You end up cutting off options.
As you plan step one, two, three, there is a specific step that might be four.
Start steps too quickly, other ways for one, two and three may not appear.

The first third of any brainstorming session is really easy.
Just come up with lots of ideas.
The second third is challenging - go through ideas and see where they lead.
Then push yourself to think a little bit outside the box.
That's often where the big idea is!
That's where the most powerful way of getting a project done fastest - is.

Most people never get to that level and short-change themselves.
Then their project takes longer and they also set up to procrastinate.
This final brainstorming part of the equation is incredibly important.

Once fully brainstormed put your options into a linear sequence.
Then you can figure out what you've overlooked.
Everything becomes obvious as you get your tasks in order.
Now add missing steps and you have laid out your task list for this project.

When you've organized the tasks into a linear process decide:
What things can you start immediately?
What can be started that are not dependent on what occurred before them?
Obviously that is step one.
There might be step five, six or twenty that don't rely on anything else to do.
You can get started on them right away too.

Now use a folder.
Write things you think of at the time and also cross off things as you do them.
Add in stuff that is relevant from time to time.

INDEX: SUCCESSFUL SELLING.

SUPPORT:

Australian Artist magazine – magazine for Australian artists

Clipping Path Universe – for photo-shop editing

Cherri Computers – for computer hardware, software printers

International Artist magazine – magazine for artists

1. Sell scientifically.

Reviewed by Susan Ashbrook - (Ottawa, Canada)
1. Are you at the starting gates?
2. On eBay you can easily analyse auction results.
3. Do market research BEFORE actually selling.
4. What are other art sellers doing?
5. Review specific listings.
6. Testing improves every aspect of your art business.
7. What stats to track.
8. Test ten critical elements for maximum profit.

1. Are you at the starting gates?

Are artistic skills enough?
Artistic skills do **NOT** decide success.
Someone without these shouldn't be trying to make a professional career.
But many artists do have those and are still not successful.

Finance is for success in any field, including professional artist.
You can't get into any business without finance nor stay in business either.
Being a professional artist is absolutely no different.
An artist who can't afford to frame paintings cannot be a professional artist.
Instead spend time raising finance from which to launch a sustained career.

The odds are stacked against success.
Of all paintings painted, most are **NEVER** sold!
This doesn't mean you can't make it.
It does mean you must well organised and clear headed about what you do.
You will battle against many alternatives someone can spend $ you want.
It's a tough world out there!
You need determination, courage, persistence, imagination, planning, help.

The good news is it can be done.
There are artists who earn a living, and you can join them - it won't be easy!
There are advantages in using eBay at the start of a career.
The main one is you can learn to sell while still learning other career aspects.
EBay provides you with all the easy-to-use tools you need to get started.

If necessary create experimental studies especially to sell on eBay.
You can list your items for auction and start selling right away.
You have to learn two things - how eBay works AND how to sell on eBay.

Use this knowledge to sell off eBay and also actual works on eBay.
It's much better than a website.
An extra $1,000 a month beats a long-shot any day of the week!

EBay changes how it works from time to time.
In this book I provide the best advice that I had at the time of writing (2010).
Almost surely there will have been changes since.
But it is likely these have been designed to make the system easier to use.
So it's important to ensure you're following eBay's official seller regulations.
Then you can stay on their good side.

EBay is great if you don't have much money to spend up front.
It only costs a dollar or two to set up a regular eBay auction listing.
You can get a steady, reliable source of income.

Using eBay is great if you want to start making money RIGHT AWAY!
Get your items listed on eBay and start making money **TODAY**, if you want.
You won't make a million dollars overnight.
But you can achieve a dependable stream of income in a very short time.

As a way of learning to sell it's hard to beat.
That's why eBay has a lot going for it for the new professional artist.
But eventually it is just another way to sell what you do.
Then choose from your own gallery, a commission based career, or eBay.

Many artists try to learn how to sell but don't actually sell anything.
That's impossible so if a selling price remained at $5 it could be worthwhile.
But of course an important part of selling is to be able to raise your price.
You can only learn this from a low starting base.

Professional artists must start selling artworks somewhere.
EBay provides the perfect place to learn sales and marketing strategies.
As your prices are still low you can't lose much while you learn.
EBay is the answer to many people's prayers – low cost and quick return.
Begin a career, learn to paint, increase productivity, actually sell, all at once.
You can even use eBay to develop a "regular" online business.
It lets you grow an opt-in list of people before a website is even running!
There's a chance to grow an opt-in list you can sell other products to.

In addition eBay is an excellent place to do valuable market research.
Then you know what your potential buyers are buying and why!

Drive thousands of interested buyers to your site the day you launch it!
These are people you've found on the world's largest marketplace.
That means they're enthusiastic online shoppers!
They're exactly the kind of people you want to introduce your works to.

To be a successful eBay seller make it part of your weekly routine.
Leave time to experiment, create listings, and prepare sold items to ship.
None of these take a huge amount of time.
But they MUST be done consistently if you want your eBay business to work.

2. On eBay you can easily analyse auction results.

Ask these questions regularly.
What parts of the auction went smoothly?
Where did I have some problems?
Were there many questions from potential bidders?
Did my description provide enough detail?
Did my auction get a lot of visitors compared to other similar ones?
How high did my item rank in the search listings?
How many bidders did I get?
How well did my sales techniques work?
What techniques failed?
Did any technique actually turn out better than I thought they would?
Were my photographs adequate?
Did the work arrive at the buyer undamaged?
Did I receive positive or negative feedback?
What would I do differently next time?

The bidders will help you.
Check emails from potential buyers in eBay email account - My Messages.
Is there a pattern of similar questions?
You may need to include answers to those questions in future listings.
You can also answer general questions in your FAQ feature.
At the start you answer emails individually but eventually there are too many.

How many visitors did your auction get?
Set up a visitor counter so you see it but it's NOT visible on your eBay site.
If you only receive a few visitors the problem is the site.
Write better titles in future.
Is the listing in the right category?

How many bids did you get?
More bids = Better price.
Click the Bids link on the Completed Item page.
OR click History on your My eBay page.

If you get lots of visitors but few bids check your product description.
Improve this with your next auction.

3. Do market research BEFORE actually selling.

Market based research.
EBay has many tools but just use two of these to keep things manageable.
Use eBay Category Listings and eBay Hot Categories Reports.

Category Listings:
Go to http://listings.ebay.com
The number of items in each category tells you how popular a category is.
Every category has a sub-category with more as they become more specific.
This process **BUYERS** use to get to something that might interest them.

Choose an appropriate category for the items you plan to sell.
In Search Option click Completed Listings, then Show Items.
Look at the number of bids to get an idea of popularity.
The amount bid or most common fixed price shows what people will spend.
Look also at how sellers write product descriptions.
Do they try to see how tough opposition is likely to be?

Study this information:
Compare sellers and analyse why one listing works better than another.
Is it the description, starting price, or whole presentation?

Hot Categories Reports.
Go to http://pages.ebay.com/sellerscentral/hotitems.pdf
Super-hot category has bids increasing at a greater rate than listing.
Demand is increasing faster than supply.

Study how other sellers sold their items.
See what approach gains highest price.
Look at what didn't sell to learn from seller mistakes.
Check opposition listings.
Find an auction by that seller click View seller's other auctions.
Check Completed Listings button.

The top eBay stores.
Go to eBay Pulse at http://pulse.ebay.com
The top stores by active listings.
Maybe buy a couple of cheap things?
Check how they do things.
What can you learn?
View the top 10 listings in each category.

The most popular products:
Go to http://product-index.ebay.com/best_selling_1.html
Items are listed in order of popularity.

Popular keywords:
Go to http://buy.ebay.com
Keywords give you an idea of what people are looking for.
Browse the most popular keywords.
Look for keywords that go with your stuff.
http://keyword-indix.ebay.com/B-1.html for keywords (blue painting).
Find specific products at http://product-keyword.ebay.com/PB-1.html

4. What are other art sellers doing?

There are many other people who are selling artworks.
Find out what they are doing.
Copy their best strategies.

Do keyword searches for words and phrases.
Don't forget Store search too for the serious seller.
Go to www.ebay.com and click Advanced Search (on right).
Do a Completed Listings search on similar items.

Specify results ranked from highest price.
These listings sold for the most money.
Write down seller ID's for people selling similar stuff to you.
What is your opposition doing wrongly?

Research your opposition artists (or galleries).
Type in name of an item (painting) you want to research.
Scroll down results page under yellow navigation bar.
Go to the left to Matching eBay Stores and Click See all Matching Stores.

Click top store and then work your way down the list:
Click first listing.
Find Meet the Seller (right side) and click List link next to View Sellers / Other Items.
Then type name of item again in the search box above the listings.
EBay will search for that item only within that seller's listings.

Check number of active auctions for that item.
Go to Completed Listings on left yellow navigation bar under Search Options.
Click Show Items button at bottom.
Result is completed listings for that seller for past 14 days for that item.
Take some notes and check other listings.

Check Meet the Seller:
Write down their User ID (for later reference).
Look for their DSR
Their feedback rating.
How long they have been a member.

Check also their feedback score in the feedback comments.
That these are in feedback comments.

Are they Power Sellers?
Do they have an About Me page?
Do they have an external website?
How many active listing do they have?
Do they specialize?
Do they ship internationally?
What payment do they accept?

5. Review specific listings.

Click ID number of a top seller.
Find items of interest - look at one and analyse what made it successful.

Look at their item (artwork).
What kind was it - is it something you don't sell?
Which characteristics seem to sell best (colour etc.)?

What is their listing category?
Is it in a category you have considered?
Is it more easily searchable than one you use?

What kind of listing/auction format do they use?
Are they using the 'Buy it Now' format?
What time of day do they seem to list their items?
How long do the auctions last?

What keywords are they using in their title?
Are they bolding any words?
What is the order of their words?
Most important - What stands out in the title?

What benefits or features are mentioned first in their headline?
Which keywords are they using?

Are they using a traditional sales-copy format?
What kind of description have they created?
How do their potential clients' questions get answered?

What stands out in their photo?
Have they positioned or staged their item?

What is their price?
If using the Buy It Now listing what is the price set at?
If the auction format what is the minimum bid?

What is their eBay store like?
What cross-promotional tools do they use?
Do they sell stuff different from yours?

Does their shipping policy differ from yours?
Is shipping discounted?

Are they shipping worldwide?
What is their return policy?

Consider their feedback ratings and DSR.
Are their clients happy?
How do they deal with negative feedback?

How do they build their relationships?
Do they have a newsletter?
Are there any written reviews or guides to take traffic to their listings?

What is their About Me page like?
What kind of pictures or text is here?
How do they establish credibility?
How do they establish trust?

6. Testing improves every aspect of your art business.

On eBay testing can help you:
Increase your visitor to bid ratio.
Increase the overall selling success of your works.
Increase the number of watchers.
Increase your client base and traffic.
Increase profits.

Lessons learned by testing can translate to other areas of your career.
Just it's easier to do within an eBay framework.
Assume nothing and test everything.
Most tests fail BUT you learn and keep testing.

Eventually a winning solution is found AND you know why.
Testing works best if you are selling the same or similar stuff.
That's why the small exercises are just right.
If necessary create special works just for eBay selling!

Use practice pieces to test buyer reaction to elements of your works.
It's a training ground - you get paid - sometimes well - for practice pieces.

It's a wonderful way to kick off a career. (Mike Barr–Adelaide, Australia)
It was a training ground - 300 or 400 beach painting taught me many things.
The most important of these was speed.
It has also given me many contacts both in Australia and overseas.
Can say sold to US, UK, Bermuda, Hong Kong, Germany. (Mike Barr–Aust.)

Change only ONE thing at a time.
Be scientific try other people's ideas - test and track a single variable.
Then you know exactly what caused any changed result.

Begin by having a control auction – your base for comparisons.
Try 3 or 4 different versions of a listing and use the best result as a control.
THEN only change **ONE** thing at a time so you can learn.

Test same listing but different title.
This simple change can produce dramatic results.

Look for more people clicking through to your description.
There should be an increase in sales or more likely price.
If this isn't the case you may be attracting people who aren't interested.
Then keep refining your title until more right people (bidders) are attracted.

Test the same listing but different description.
If you think you have the right people but sales haven't improved.
Then the product description isn't working well enough.
You may need extra stuff to convince a prospect your offer is a good one.
You also need to explain why prospects should buy from you.
Show how you are trustworthy as well.

It should NOT be just a description – in spite of the name.
The job of the description is to **SELL**.
This is your most powerful selling tool.

Test the same listing but different starting bids.
Start at 99c – which could be your control.
Then try a start that covers your costs.
Which generates the best profit?
Remember the higher start also raises your eBay listing fee.
Test Buy It Now and various reserve prices too.

7. What stats to track.

Track the elements of your listing.
Maintain detailed records of your eBay transactions.
This will give instant feedback AND long-term trend identification.
Get this information from you're my eBay page.
Sell many works get eBay's Sales Reports Plus (free) weekly and monthly.

Track the number of visitors to your auction.
Here study the effect of your Title, Gallery Photo and any Listing Upgrades.
Listing upgrades are things like bold type, highlights or borders.
Find the best combination of these elements that attracts most visitors.
Then focus on your description and starting price.
Make sure your profit margin isn't reduced.

Track the conversion rate.
Getting visitors is one thing but getting a good price is another.
Your Product Description is the major influence (sales copy).
Starting Bid and photo quality have an effect too.

Test each of these elements separately over a period of time.
The conversion rate of visitors to bids is a key statistic.
Number of bids/Number of Visitors x 100 = Visitor to Bid conversion rate.
A higher rate means you are attracting the right visitors and they are bidding.
Visitors could mean the same few people a number of times.
If happy again focus on the description to attract even more prospects.

Track your sell-through rate.
This is the % of listings that are sold.
The important sell-through rate is YOURS.
Constantly aim to improve this by applying the best of your tests.

Use tracking tools.
Develop a tracking spreadsheet.
See sample elsewhere.
Use eBay's Sales Reports – go to
http://pages.ebay.com/salesreports/welcome/html .
Compare results against your targets.

Understand the main drivers of your business.
Select opportunities and areas for improvement.
Generally refine your business strategy.
You should probably use Sales Reports rather than Sales Reports Plus.

8. Test ten critical elements for maximum profit.

Test your offer which is what you are selling – the total package.
Make changes by varying different benefits or including a bonus.
Perhaps you could offer free shipping?
Measure visitor to bid ratio, compare ending price, compare average price.

Test your auction title which initially captures a prospect's attention.
Don't forget to use keywords.
Test for keywords, different sizes, colours, subjects, style, medium,
Measure the number of visitors, the Best Match listing placement.

Test any subtitles.
Use them in specific places – incentive free shipping, different times of year.
Do people then click to your description?
Measure the number of visitors.

Test features (bold, border, highlight).
Test carefully **BEFORE** using these as you have to pay for them.
Run with and without these and compare the results.
Measure the number of visitors.

Test the effect of Gallery Plus.
Gallery Plus is an enlarged version of your gallery image.

With a painting it could be worth the extra money.
It must increase your final price or your sales volume.
Measure the number of visitors.

Test product description (sales copy) - add testimonials, move photos.
Experiment with your benefits, formatting, design and layout, placement of
images, call to action, cross-promotion, bonus descriptions, and long versus
short sales copy.
Measure visitor to bid ratio, ending prices, compare to average prices.
You can't determine best strategy without testing.
Then you know what to do.
With artworks there is an argument to start higher to provide perceived value.
Measure visitors, visitor to bid conversion ratio, Best Match listing place.

Test number of photos.
See if the number of photos has any effect.
Assume nothing but test by measuring the visitor to bid conversion rate.

Test duration and timing of your auctions.
Test different auction lengths with attention on the first and last few hours.
Try different times and different days.
Measure the number of visitors, visitor to bid conversion ratio, ending price.

Test design elements in your description.
Check the effect of different fonts and colours.
Can your visitors easily read your listing?
Measure visitor to bid conversion rate, ending price.

2. Sell logically.

Reviewed by Mike Barr = (Adelaide, Australia)
1. Your eBay profile.
2. Start to sell by buying.
3. Feedback ratings.
4. Selling strategies.
5. Ways to limit your focus.

1. Your eBay profile.

When you register you will need to create an eBay user ID.
Your clients and prospects will read this but you can change your ID later.
If you have a company then that could be used but it is not essential.
It's a good idea if the ID conveys something to your prospective clients.
"Joebloggsoilpainting" could be the kind of thing.

You will need a password which only you need to know.
You will be sent an email, respond and that completes registration.

Download the eBay toolbar.
Click the **DOWNLOAD** button.
Double click the file you save as a result of downloading.
Click Sign in for advanced features and register there too.
Click Customize to change the set up to suit your own tastes.

There is so much stuff on eBay you should spend time book-marking.
Then you can find what you want quickly and easily.
Keep adding new pages to this folder as you discover them.
Use the Internet Explorer Favourites button rather than eBay Favourites.

Start by book-marking these pages.
New to eBay which helps you get started.
EBay Site Map which helps locate pages.
Learning Centre: instructions, video tours, tutorials, buying, selling, feedback.

A to Z index to find stuff by subject and key word searches.
My eBay to find it after you sign in as it is the hub of **YOUR** eBay business.
Seller Central for selling tips in product categories.
Advanced Search uses key words, categories, sellers, prices, location, bids.
EBay My World to customize your profile and share it with other users.
Customize the look and feel of your pages as well.

Set up a free PayPal account.
Personal account which can accept only PayPal payments.
Premier account is recommended.
This allows acceptance of credit cards.
Small % charge of amount received.
Flat fee $.30US per transaction.

Business account:
Best if you have an established business with a bank account.

How to set up PayPal account.
Go to www.paypal.com
Click Sign Up at top of page.
Select country and language.

Choose personal, premier or business account.
Click Start Now.
Enter personal information as on your bank account.
Email address and password will be used to log in to your PayPal account.
Recommended you use a different password from your eBay account.
Choose two security questions and answers.
Enter characters at the bottom of your screen as you see them.
Select I agree Create My Account after read user agreement, privacy policy.

Check your email address.
Find PayPal message and click the link.
Return to PayPal site enter password and you now have a PayPal account.

Protect your account.
Emails from eBay show in eBay My Messages inbox as well as your own.
An eBay or PayPal message will address you by your first name.
No name = false BUT even with a name an email may not be genuine.
If the URL looks unusual and is not the standard eBay or PayPal URL.
Your eBay toolbar account guard turns **RED** when you click a fake email.
Your eBay toolbar account guard turns **GREEN** if you click a genuine email.
The eBay toolbar account guard is **GREY** if you aren't using eBay or PayPal.

For more information:
Visit www.paypal.com/security.
Or http://pages.ebay.com/education/spooftutorial/index.html.

Problems when buying on eBay:
Take care of sellers with bad feedback check at www.toolhaus.org .

If it looks too good to be true particularly for one day auctions.
Then it could be stolen goods or fake goods for sale.
Seller's friends drive up the price (look out for retracted high price bids).
Only buy using eBay facilities.

2. Start to sell by buying.

Selling via eBay could help an artist commence their career.
Mike Barr provided me with this idea that I didn't have previously.
Start by looking at different auction strategies.
Buy it now pricing.
Low starting bids.
Highlighting listings on the search results page.
Using different numbers or styles of images.
Techniques that make you want to bid are likely to work with other people.
Use them in your own listings.

Pick something you'd like to buy (not expensive).
Look for it on sale.
Consider **WHY** you do everything in the process of finding a listing.
What is appealing about certain auctions?
What draws your eye to a listing?
What persuades you to make a bid?
What do you want to know but can't find out?

Are you ready to bid?
Click Place Bid below the current bid at the top.
Enter your maximum bid and wait.
Most bidding takes place in the final few minutes of an auction.
So bid late rather than early.
Say you win an auction.
Carefully note how the checkout process works.
When you receive the item leave feedback for the seller.
You can leave an anonymous DSR (Detailed Seller Rating).
Record your impressions in your Ideas Book (maybe a special eBay version).
Did the item meet your expectations as described in the listing?
Did the seller email you after the auction?
How long did it take to arrive?
Were extra charges fair?
If the process was good then copy it yourself later.

3. Feedback ratings

Feedback ratings are the core of eBay.
Your feedback IS your credibility on eBay.
Start as a buyer to establish credibility **AND** make payments on time.
Leave feedback when you receive whatever you bought.
ASK for positive feedback which is OK on eBay.

It doesn't matter what you buy if it's enough to build your feedback.
Go to your My eBay page Click Feedback in left column under My Account.
Click Leave Feedback to reveal page with items you bought.
Choose Positive, Neutral or Negative feedback.
Make sure descriptions are read carefully to avoid mistakes and problems.
If something goes wrong contact the seller first and explain the problem.
Most sellers will fix problem to avoid negative feedback.
It is possible to change your feedback.

There are THREE parts of your feedback profile.
The Feedback Score (a number shown in brackets).
A Positive Feedback Percentage (just underneath).
The Detailed Seller Ratings (a system of stars).

After every transaction buyers are encouraged to leave feedback.
They have 60 days to do this.
They can leave positive score +1, neutral score 0, or negative score -1.
They can write one line to explain their score.
Complete the DSR to provide a ranking out of 5 stars in four different areas.
Your score is the total number of feedback points in last 12 months.
Negative AND neutral points are deducted from positive points.
Positive Feedback % is the number of positive points as a % of all feedback.
Different coloured **STAR** symbols show your feedback ranking.
View stars go to http://pages.ebay.com/help/feedback/reputation-stars.html

Detailed Seller Rankings (DSR) ARE important.
They help decide listing position on eBay searches.
Decide eligibility to be a power seller.
Can save money on fees.
DSR 5 rating means there were no problems.
It doesn't mean going to superhuman lengths.

Did they receive what you described?
Was there anything misleading?

Communication:
Was seller (you) easy to contact?
Were you willing to answer questions?
Were you friendly and professional?

Was it shipped in the time frame promised?
Was it sent the way it was advertised?
Were shipping and handling charges reasonable?
Did they reflect the actual cost of packaging and delivering the artwork?

Building your feedback scores.
Start by becoming a buyer.
Buy some low cost items on eBay.
Packaging to send your artwork could be a start.
Make your payments on time and be friendly and courteous.
Leave positive feedback when transaction has concluded.
Ask seller to return the favour.

Build your rating.
Complete as many transactions as you can.
Buy and sell small and inexpensive items to start with.
Ship the works quickly.
Make sure you ask for feedback for every transaction you do well.

Be the seller you buy from professional and courteous at all times.
Respond quickly to emails and enquiries and ship promptly and carefully.
Resolve disputes or misunderstandings quickly and know a client **IS** right.
Encourage contact if not 100% happy as buyers can reverse their feedback.

Use your About Me and My World pages.
Share information about yourself and your experience.
Tell of other activities like website or gallery but don.t provide direct links.

Know your legal obligations.
For policy overview go to http://pages.ebay.comhelp/policies/overview.html
Sellers rules: http://pages.ebay.comhelp/policies/seller-rules-overview.html
For feedback rules: http://pages.ebay.comhelp/policies/feedback-ov.html

When selling ask for feedback because good feedback is worth money.
Good eBay feedback scores earn 8% more than new sellers with same item.
It also determines where your listing appears in the rankings.

Ask for feedback whenever possible and build a positive rating.
Show a large number of responses to show you are experienced.
With Detailed Seller Ratings you get better placement in eBay search results.
You'll get some fee reductions as well.
All you have to do is ask nicely.

Respond to buyers quickly and ship quickly.
Provide feedback for your buyers.
After you receive the money and sent your work also send an email.
Say you have sent the work and tell them when they can expect to receive it.
Thanks them for their support and remind them to leave feedback.

Wait until you are certain a buyer is satisfied THEN leave feedback.
If there is no buyer feedback then send an email asking if everything is OK.
Once buyer has left positive feedback return the favour.

Here are ways good feedback helps if you also have a PayPal account.
One sale with or without feedback you can open your own store.

Without PayPal a Feedback rating of 20 is needed.
5 positive feedback ratings you can sell at a fixed price using Buy It.
No PayPal = 10.
10 positive feedback rating you can use Best Offer on single-item listings.

You can also buy Featured Plus.
If ID verified previous two options are available.
15 positive feedback rating can sell multiple copies of an item in a single list.
Use Multiple Item Listing (no PayPal = 50).Â
20 positive feedback rating can open eBay Store without an eBay account.
30 positive feedback rating can accept Best Offers on a Multiple Item Listing.

Must have had eBay account for 14 days or be ID verified.
100 positive feedback rating with Positive Feedback of 98% items.
Can be listed on eBay Express (www.express.ebay.com).

Become a Power Seller.
You will be invited to join when qualified.
100 positive feedback keep 98% of sales of $1000 for 3 consecutive months.
Also maintain a rating of 4.5 or higher for past 12 months in ALL four DSR's.

Then you can access.
Power seller icon shows potential buyers you meet eBay's high standards.

Welcome kit which shares advanced selling tips.
Priority support from eBay.
Networking opportunities.
Special offers.

Final Value discounts from 5% to 20% depending on your DSR.
Increased visibility in Best Match searches.

4. Selling strategies

There are basically two approaches to selling anything.
High volume, low-profit sales BUT you MUST sell a lot.
Low volume, high profit sales BUT you must sell.
Either way can be profitable.

Selling low-priced high volume works.
Your main problem is to produce them.
BUT use experimental studies and you will have stock.
You will need to run more auctions BUT this IS good training.
You can group several works and sell as a package.
Profit margins can be small.
Decide by sorting results of market research by price.
What are the average prices for stuff in categories like yours?

Selling high-priced low volume works.
Success depends on your profit margin.
An artist usually sells a low cost product so this strategy is very attractive.
BUT you will need to establish credibility as a seller.

People do not pay high prices without seller credibility.
Product descriptions will need to be accurate and comprehensive.
Negative feedback will need to be avoided.
Often fewer people are looking to buy.

Give it a try if you have you had an experience like this?
Had a solo show at a local gallery but now owe $$$ in spite of two sales?
There is still quite a collection of artworks to sell.
Framing is expensive although they look wonderful all hanging at the gallery.

It is possible to make between $500 and $1000 on eBay every week.
There are artists that do.
BUT it took a long time to establish a following and consistent flow of works.
You should have at least one painting for auction at any one time.

Sell a low cost item to start with Mike Barr (Adelaide Australia).
Sell off unsold works quickly as a way of clearing stock.

Your experimental studies are an ideal beginning too.
Sold unframed they will be easy to pack and ship.
You will be less likely to have negative feedback or DSR's.
On the other hand just create affordable original works.

Mike has made brand new works and introduced them on eBay.
There's a whole truckload of painters doing that and enjoying the process.

They call themselves "daily painters".
They do work every day on a particular piece.
Once they finish the artwork they post it right away in eBay.
Others paint a small artwork daily so everyday there's a new painting offered.

As you gain experience gradually feel out the higher priced market.
Eventually your career will be built on that selling strategy.
BUT at the start it is very difficult or even impossible.

Making a profit is what selling is all about!
The reality is you MUST make a profit (sale price - expenses = profit/loss).
So you should know the price your works are likely to sell for.
Then you know how much you can spend on production and eBay fees.
EBay's main charges are Insertion Fees and Final Value Fees.
Go to www.ebcalc.com for the eBay Fee Calculator to get an exact figure.

Insertion Fees are insurance.
They guarantee you will not sell for less than the starting fee you pay for.

Starting low attracts the bargain hunters and gets bidding started.
Starting at .99c costs 15c to 20c less than starting at $1!
Test what happens with some low priced works.

Final Value Fee:
The more you pay the better your selling price was.
These fees are **MUCH** lower than galleries and art shows charge per sale.
The higher your selling price the lower your % fee.

Optional Fees:
Reserve fees.
Buy It Now fees.
Listing Upgrade fees.
EBay Picture Services fee.
Selling Tool fees.
Use **ONLY** if you believe you can attract more bidders and/or higher price.
Test carefully before spending on optional fees.

Know your margin BEFORE you sell in quantity.
Understanding margin is crucial actual profit = Gross income per sale - costs.

Costs = production cost:

eBay Listing fee, eBay Final Value fee, PayPal or Credit Card fee, shipping. Your income is the Final Selling Price and the Shipping and handling fee,

An example:

Your small painting actually cost $5 in materials.
A starting price of $0.99 costs $0.10.
You actually sell the painting for $10 + $5 for shipping.
EBay charges a Final Value Fee of $0.88.
PayPal charges $0.75.
The actual mailing cost is $3.75.
You buy a cardboard cylinder to mail your work in - cost $0.20.

Your profit on this sale:

($10 + $5) â€" ($2 + $0.10 + $0.88 + $0.75 + $3.80 + $0.20) = $7.27
That is almost 50%.

Use www.ebcalc.com to help you with your calculations.

For more comprehensive calculations
use www.nortica.com/UserArea/EPC.aspx

5. Ways to increase your profit.

Increase your profit by increasing your final selling price.
Write benefit rich descriptions.
Use better photos.
Lower shipping charges.
Add free bonuses.

Increase your profit by decreasing production costs.
Buy materials in bulk.
Use cheaper materials for here they don't need to be conservation standard.
Work faster so you have more works to sell from a given amount of time.

Increase your profit by decrease eBay listing fees.
List as part of special promotions.
Be frugal with your add-ons.
Use templates where possible.
Host pictures elsewhere to avoid eBay picture fees.

Increase profit by decreasing final value fess.
Price base for Buy It Now, Reserve Pricing, eBay Stores, and auctions.
Which has highest rate of return and lowest fees?

Increase your profit by decreasing credit card fees.
Use PayPal preferred to save 1% sign up for a merchant account.

Increase your profit by using rewards.
PayPal debit/credit card or eBay MasterCard offer rewards.
You can use these rewards against your fees.

Increase your profit by decreasing shipping costs.
Use smallest package possible.
Use padded or plastic envelopes instead of boxes.
Research all options at your post office.
Buy shipping materials in bulk.

Increase your profit by increasing your shipping fee charges.
Charge a fair price to cover not just shipping but cost of packing **AND** time.
Keep in line with other sellers to avoid penalties.

Choose the most effective auction format!
There are four listing formats (online, Fixed Price, Store, and Classified Ads).

The auction duration can be 1, 3, 5, 7, or 10 days.
Longer auctions are better for artwork.
Because prospects like to watch and think.
If you are linking with Christmas then there needs to be enough time to ship.

Probably a 7 or 10 day listing is best for art.
A 10 day listing will cost an extra 40c which could be OK for two week-ends.

Reserve Price should be used for very high priced and limited market.
Buy It Now if someone bids the BIN price the auction ends.
Set a low starting price with a higher BIN price draws in bargain hunters.

Get quick sales with higher starting price and a BIN price a little more.
BIN pricing is good for holidays when people want stuff quickly.

Fixed Price Listing
These are **NOT** auctions.
Need a good inventory, know what people will pay, know your profit margin.

Store Listing
You can display all your listings exclusively in your store.
Generally listed at a set price.
Listing fees are lower but final value fees are higher.
Subtitle is cheaper and listing upgrades last 30 days.
Store listings can have an unlimited duration.
You can add Best Offer.
Generally less visibility in eBay searches.
Good when you have some eBay experience.

Classified Ad Listing.
These are NOT auctions.
Sales take place outside the eBay setup.
Only available for certain categories.
Go to http://pages.ebay.com/help/sell/adformatfees.html#list
For more information Go to http://pages.ebay.com/help/sell/f-ad.html

Add upgrades with CARE.
Upgrades ALL cost money so it is easy for fees to get out of control.
Thus they reduce your profit unless they increase your sales.

A gallery picture is FREE so use it.
Down the track Gallery Plus could be considered.

Bolding is OK if it increases your profit.

Highlighting is also OK if it increases your profit but it IS expensive.

Border is OK if it increases your profit.
Subtitle is only 50c to entice prospects to click your auction.
Breaks up pattern of the search and allows extra details to be added.

Use price to start the bidding.
How much risk will you take?
Start **LOW** and you will generate bids **BUT** you **MAY** sell cheaply.
Research completed listing for other similar artworks.
What were their starting bids?

A lower starting bid attracts a lower initial listing fee.
You are more likely to attract early bidders and get the auction rolling.
Possibly initially you could start at the lowest price you will accept.
BUT you could turn some bidders away.

Reserve Price strategies.
Later you may want to sell your work for a higher price (**NOT** PP painting).
Then start the bidding at the lowest price you will take.
Set a Fixed Price and use the Best Offer option to find what people will pay.
The Fixed Price could be higher than you want.

Sell prints and sell cheap.
Have lots of different prints.
More you have the more you sell.
Having many means the money adds up.
You can reduce cost by sending image by email.

What is the best auction TIME?
Most bids for most auctions come in the final few minutes.
People don't place bids earlier to avoid driving the price up.
You want maximum numbers viewing the final few minutes to get best price.

Generally eBay traffic is highest at week-ends.
It is also busy during the week from 5pm to 9pm (after work).
Art buyers probably are most common at these times too.
Research other art sellers and see what they are doing.
Check the time eBay operates on, it may be US Pacific Time.

What are your REAL costs?
Your time is the main hidden cost.
Artists rarely think of their time as a cost.
How many paintings do you do in a year?
If you painted faster could you double this?
What if your standard stayed the same?
What would be the result for your income?

You normally paint 20 paintings in a year.
You can produce at least 200 PP paintings/studies/sketches.
You normally sell 5 paintings a year (25%).
If you sell 50 PP paintings at 10% normal price you gross the same money.
Perhaps you sell 25 PP paintings at 20% of the normal price?
There are many options available including some that make more money.

BUT the PP paintings can cover your time spent.
You spend **MUCH** less time on each painting.
Calculate the cost of that time and include it in your price.
The high price low volume approach is taken up in other places.

Selling on eBay is a great way to learn to sell at the start of a career!
Another **REAL** cost is the time taken to list stuff on eBay.
In the beginning this will be considerable as you are learning what to do.
Later you are faster but always takes time so sales **MUST** pay for that time.
In future your costs could include the cost of studio and store room.
When you are really successful your stock will need to build up.
It costs real money to convert a garage, spare bedroom or rent somewhere.

What is your stuff actually worth?
Check other auctions selling stuff like yours but online rather than eBay.
Test out different pricing strategies to find the highest return.
Aim to continually improve your profit margin.

Include photographs of anything that will indicate worth.
Your signature on the painting as well as a date.
The right photo is worth $$$.

Value can change according to the season.
There is a strong demand at Christmas for gifts.
Your PP paintings fall into this category.
Save them for then and you will get a higher price than a month or so later.

Create a product to fill a market gap.
Your PP paintings are now designed to fill a market gap identified on eBay.
The gap will be linked to the focus required.
A T shirt with one of your works printed could be an eBay sale item.

Advertise your eBay listing.
This might be on your Facebook page.
Also any other social media you are involved with.
The more people who you what you have the better result you'll get.

3. Start small.

Reviewed by: Renee Ruggles – (Arena, Wisconsin)

1. Limit your focus!
2. Avoid misunderstandings.
3. Deal with negative feedback and gain a satisfied client.
4. Photographs
5. Creating a listing
6. Payment and shipping

1. Limit your focus.

Focus on one media, certain subject, particular size, whatever.
People get to know you because of your focus.
They will share that focus with you.

Sell your cheap PP studies before you even think of major works.
Even then only start with a few studies for you must learn first.
Then you'll be able to understand your market and pricing trends.
You'll also write better descriptions than your opposition.

Use your DSR score to get a BEST MATCH listing.

Prevent bad seller experiences BEFORE they happen!
How often key words get clicked on by buyers.
Listings with most clicked key words considered more relevant.

Buyer dissatisfaction.
Rates of more than 5% in last 30 days = lower listings.

Low DSRs for shipping and handling.
Means decreased exposure.
DSR above 4.7% in all four categories in last 30 days.
Along with 98% positive feedback = higher ranking.
This could give 20% more exposure than for a comparable item.

Shipping costs significantly above average in same sub-category.
May receive reduced exposure.
Time remaining for auction is considered but not main criteria.

To get a HIGH DSR score.
Give your buyers what they expect.
Main reason for negative feedback is not getting what was expected.

Put your work in the right category.
Most people do this.
Sometimes eBay changes and sub-categories may then vary.

Describe a work as accurately as possible.
Don't leave out anything a buyer might want to know.
Dimensions, media, frame (or not), etc.

Clearly describe any flaws.
Maybe there is a tear on one edge?

Pictures will help you sell, particularly artwork on eBay.
Use as many photos as necessary – which might be just one.
Show any flaws, blemishes, wear marks, with close-ups.
Show the date and signature with a close up.
Be accurate and honest.

Specify shipping details.
Include shipping service, cost and packing.
Put this information in the details of your listing **AND** the description.

Anticipate and respond to ALL client questions in your description.
Develop a FAQ and post it in your Answers section of the eBay help for sellers' page.

Offer a Money Back Guarantee.
A warranty shows your confidence about what you are selling.
Your goal is to make the buyer happy – no matter what!
Make sure you state who is responsible for return shipping charges.

Deliver on ALL promises.
Start the bidding at a price you are willing to accept.
Set a low initial price but sometimes it will sell low too.
Include shipping and return policies in the listing as well as policies page.
Follow them to the letter.

2. Avoid misunderstandings.

Be crystal clear about everything.
Make sure your item description is not confusing so avoid arty language.
Clearly state shipping and return policies where they can be seen.

Use eBay Messages and auto-responders.
Update your clients regularly.
When you receive payment.
When you ship their painting.
Leave them positive feedback.

Use personal email to add greetings etc.
Make sure they have received your work.

Answer emails promptly.
The free eBay toolbar notifies when emails arrive so deal with problems immediately.

Add a personal touch.
Include a short thank-you with the painting although a free surprise is better.
Send a follow-up to see if everything arrived OK.

Go the extra mile.
List the four DSR criteria in a client service section of your auction.
Under each heading show exactly how you address each of these areas.
Point people to specific feedback that praises you in those areas.

Ask for five star DSR's.
Include a note with a painting ask for positive feedback and top stars - like:
I value your business and am committed to making you 100% satisfied.
If you're happy with the purchase, leave me positive feedback and five stars.
I will return the favour.
If I've fallen short, give me a chance to make it right before feedback.

Post items promptly.
Get it in the mail fast and keep the client informed at every stage.
Set up a shipping centre.
Add a day or two to your shipping times – better to arrive early than late.
Track your package if possible – let client know what is happening.
If international emphasize you post paintings as soon as you get payment.
BUT parcels can get held up in customs sometimes.

Offer competitive shipping rates.
Only charge fair and accurate shipping costs.
Look at competitor's rates.
http://pages.ebay.com/help/sell/actual-rate-example.html automatic calculate.
FREE shipping is a very attractive add-on for a potential buyer.
Offer shipping discounts for multiple purchases.
Provide details of any packaging charges – what exactly is it for?

3. Deal with negative feedback and gain a satisfied client.

Buyers can change their negative feedback.
Block high-risk buyers from your auctions.
This is possible and from time to time could be a good strategy.
Get eBay to remove abusive feedback that violates eBay policy.

There should be none of the following:
External links or scripts.
References to eBay or PayPal investigations.
Negative statements that conflict with a positive rating.
Personal information about another member.
Comments that don't have anything to do with the transaction.
Racist, vulgar or obscene comments.

EBay will remove feedback when:
There is no response to the Unpaid Item process.
A buyer or seller is suspended.

Clear up misunderstandings.
New buyers often don't understand how things work so resolve issues.
Focus on problem not person **AND** give the buyer the benefit of the doubt.

Report any troublemakers to eBay.

4. Photographs

Photographs are essential but ONE is usually enough and is free.
A camera of 2.0 mega-pixels, a macro feature (close up) and manual flash.

You need accurate photographs.
You do **NOT** need artistic photographs.
They should show your work as accurately as possible.

Photographs should answer any questions a buyer may have.
This could be with one image but sometimes more are needed.
Make sure you show the signature and date (if any).

Photos attract more bids and higher bids.
Not surprising as bidders can't actually see the real thing.
Should reinforce and enhance the words used to describe your painting.

A good image or set of images will:
Reinforce your credibility by showing bidders you actually have this work.
Increase the work's desirability by showing what it is like.
Help bidders make a decision based on what the work actually looks like.
Attract more bids by making your work look better than alternatives.
Gain the trust of bidders if any defects are shown.
Help you score high DSR's as people get what they expect.

Number of images depends on the value of the work.
Higher value = more images.
Are you paying eBay for the images?
Worth it for high value paintings.
For low value paintings one good image should be enough.

You can take professional images.
A digital camera will do the job.
Show your work from various angles if necessary.
Take up to 20 photos of the same work.
Use flash, no flash, macro-lenses, different camera settings, inside/outside.
See what works best.
Eventually you will only need to take a few photos.

Light the work and then take the photo.
Set up a small photo studio in a corner of your studio.
A couple of desk lamps can provide enough illumination.
Use halogen bulbs not fluorescent or ordinary bulbs.

Avoid flash glare.
Don't use the camera flash at all.
Take photographs of paintings **BEFORE** they go under glass.

Get close and fill the frame with the work and show the whole painting.
Most digital cameras have a micro setting for small details.
A tripod will prevent blurriness.
Show imperfections up close.

Provide a size reference.
A ruler, tape measure or common object next to the work will show its size.
Other references could be a coin, a drink can, or a pen.

Provide a colour reference.
Sometimes you need to do this and a common coloured object would do.

Eliminate any background if possible.
A background is a distraction if some shows so use a plain background.
If necessary crop your images and select only what you want to show.

Take photographs at the same time as you write.
Then it is easier to make your images consistent with your description.
It will also be easier to find the right words.

Have a clear focus.
There should be no blurry edges but a clear crisp image.
Take a number of photos so you can select the best.

5. Creating a listing

What sells on eBay?
There's **NO** difference between what sells on eBay and what sells anywhere!
To sell – someone pays money – **YES** answer is needed to these questions.

Is your stuff scarce?
Undoubtedly it is but stuff that is commonplace is hard to sell.

Is your stuff desirable?
Undoubtedly you think so **BUT** do other people?
Who is it desirable to?

Is your stuff in demand?
There's no doubt that at the start it is **NOT**.
So initially the focus has to be here.
Get **MORE** people to want your stuff.
Then you are on your way.

These factors can be a focus for your eBay marketing.
They can be a focus in your off-eBay marketing too – but it is harder to do.

Pricing should reflect these factors.
As the demand rises, so does scarcity, and your prices should match.
Again this applies on eBay and elsewhere too.
A sudden increase in demand can drive prices higher, just like the real world.
Manage these factors and money can be made on eBay.
Money can be made anywhere by managing this equation.

You might also consider what problems do artists or collectors face?
Do you have a solution you can sell?
You need to know:
What is the average selling price for similar items?
How many auctions have there been for similar items in the last 30 days?
What is the sell-through rate for similar items on eBay?

Start creating a listing.
A listing **IS** an offer BUT it could appear under several different categories.

You could use extra words in a title.
You might be very descriptive.
You could use fewer words.
Whatever you do will affect sales.

Do you have an offer for clients?
You must have an offer.
It's the most basic element of marketing.
It's the answer to this question:

Why should I buy from you…. now?
You could promote a discount, and that would be an offer.
Particularly if it was tied to a limited time frame, say, this week.
There are many other ways to make offers without discounting.

So why should anyone buy from you?
People need a reason to act.
You need to create some desire, and to be enticing.
You lead the reader to what you want them to do, bid on your artwork.
Just describing the artwork available is **NOT** enough.

Here are some ways you can do this?
Place your work in the right Category:
Go to the Sell page using Browse Categories link.
Select a category – probably art.
Check by finding similar items.
Maybe copy some stuff from those listings.

Item Specifics:
This helps eBay deliver the most relevant results to potential buyers.
Often it is filled in automatically.

Your Title is VERY important:
Use descriptive keywords and their variations.
Stick to facts and avoid adjectives.
Describe style, colour, frame, size, etc.
How would you look for this item?

The Item description is VERY IMPORTANT too.
BUT it **IS** sales copy **NOT** a description.
You can describe your work in some detail.
BUT telling a story is even better.

Put yourself in the bidder's shoes.
What would interest them?
How will your work help the bidder?
Follow any feature (description) with an explicit benefit.
This is where you can tell the bidder about yourself.

On eBay there is a need for re-assurance about your credibility.
Ask for the sale – this item won't last long!

Starting Price:
Start at 99cents.
Minimizes fees and attracts initial bidders.
Set up the first few sales as simple auction format listings.
Even sell at a very low price (well to start with).
Later use Advanced Search of completed listings.

Look at the final sale price of other items like yours.
If they didn't sell you will need to rethink your eBay strategies.

Terms and Conditions:
Payments – PayPal.
Shipping – upfront about cost and time.
Feedback.
Warranty.
Refund policy.
Be as clear as possible and as fair as possible too.
Ask them to contact you if they have any questions.
Add a call to action – Bid now!

Need help?
Visit the Sell Your Item page.
Click to the SYI form.
Automatic guide.
Can save and complete later.
Can save as templates (very handy for your artworks).

Now continue with your listing.
Once you have written the copy then use eBay's formatting options.
Go to eBay's Sell Your Item form.

Choose one or more categories.
EBay will make suggestions based on your keywords.
Use the category that gets the highest profit.

Enable pre-filled information.
BUT check that they are correct for your work.
The Item Specifics box will let you see this information.
Enter some of your details.
This is organized to make it easier for a buyer and eBay's search engine.

Edit your title and sub-title.
Make adjustment so they read a little better if necessary.
Don't lose what you have created though.

Add pictures.
For a painting this is essential.

Add a visitor counter.
Then you can check and see how many times it has been viewed.
Don't display the counter on your page as the information is just for you.

Specify delivery details.
Use eBay's Shipping Wizard.

Let's look more closely at selecting the right category.
Use eBay's Sell Your Item Form and check your work is in the right place.
Go to Sell Your Item at www.ebay.com/sell.
Type in keywords for your work in the search field.
Use words you think a buyer would use.
You get a breakdown of different categories of recently listed similar items.
You will also see the % listed in each category.

Now choose your category possibly where similar items are found.
That might be a category you might not have thought about.
Possibly list in two categories AND identify categories to avoid.
Use a keyword search.
This provides actual numbers of items in each category at that time.

Choose to be in a popular category or dominate a less used one.
Consider this if your opposition is particularly well organized.
Also use another category if a work failed to sell in your original choice.
Check completed **AND** current listings.

Adjust your choice according to the results.
A category the same as a keyword is worth listing in.
No one searches the Other category.

Think like a buyer for they buy for their own reasons.
This isn't always the same as you think so you may need to test alternatives.

Make sure your title includes keywords!
Your title is VERY important and the right keywords attract search traffic.
Over 90% of eBay visitors search by typing in key words.

A well written title catches the eye of potential buyers.
Your title **MUST** stand out to be noticed.
If people don't visit your listing then what's there just doesn't matter.

The right keywords will help get your listing seen?
Keywords are words or phrases that describe or name your painting.
They are words people type into the search box when they are looking.
Your keywords also are relevant to where your listing is seen.

What words will a buyer use?
They haven't seen your painting either!
Do a search and pay attention to what you find.

The job of the title IS to draw the right people to your listing.
There is a 55 character limit to the title.
Every single letter (and space) has to do its job.

Consider common miss-spellings and variations of words.
That's if space is available.
ALWAYS use singular rather than plurals in a title.
Use common acronyms.
EBay has a list of acronyms.
Go to Help at top of page then eBay Acronyms.
Make sure an acronym is written in full in the actual listing to avoid confusion.

Here are some you might use to save on that character limit.
BIN = Buy it now.
LE = Limited Edition
LTD = Limited
NR = No Reserve
P = Poor condition
PP = PayPal
S&H, S/H, SH = Shipping and handling.
SZ = Size

Develop your own acronyms specifically for use with your artworks.
OIL = Oil painting
WCOL = Watercolour (however spelled).
PAST = Pastel
CHAR = Charcoal.
PEN = Pen and ink.
PENC = Pencil
ETCH = Etching

LITH = Lithograph
SCR = Screen-print or serigraph
GIC = Giclee
LAND = Landscape
PORT = Portrait
SEA = Seascape
SL = Still Life
NUD = Nude or figurative

Your title doesn't need to be a proper sentence.
It's **BETTER** if it's a list of searchable keywords but if readable that's OK.
Your title **MUST** stand out from lots of other similar titles to get looked at.
Include size, artist (you), subject, medium, framing, condition, in the title.

How do you find the right keywords?
Search eBay's Completed Listings sorted by highest price.
Look at titles that attracted most bidders and highest final selling price.
http://pulse.ebay.com for top 10 search words in category and sub category.
Look at titles of chosen categories for biggest most successful eBay Stores.

Test your keywords
Find out exactly which keywords rank best in Best Match.
List your painting, note where it ranks.
Change your title and the ranking will change within five minutes.
Continue up until 12 hours before auction ends and stick to the best result.

Put keywords in key places.
Start of the title will be read by eBay before the end – so that's the best spot.
That's where what people look for goes too.

Take care with capital letters.
Don't use **ALL** capitals for that it harder to read.
DO capitalize the **FIRST** letter of **EACH** word in the **TITLE**.
All lower case tends to blend in with the search list.

A free bonus can entice more bidders.
Add + bonus or free bonus to your listing.

Test different titles and see which one works best.
The difference **CAN** be considerable!

Warning:
Messages from eBay appear in the My Messages section of your eBay page.

Ideas to generate action:
Provide advance notice of a listing, so your clients feel special.
Have time limits, so a sense of urgency - people need to act now or miss out.
Buy one get one free, or variation of combinations of works, prints or cards.
Provide easy payment terms so works are affordable and clients decide now.

Limited quantity at special price to save money by prompt action.
Have a money back guarantee to provide credibility and reassurance.
Offer free samples, workshops, information kits, to generate action.
Provide gifts and add-ons if clients respond by a certain date.

Offers work best if represent a high-perceived value for your clients.
Sketch by you is more highly regarded by your buyers than book on Picasso.
Take your time to construct an offer.
It can make a great difference to the success of your marketing campaign.
You could even test several offers if you give yourself time.
Write many different offers for your current marketing campaign.
Which means you can select the best one to test.

Improve the look of your listing.
Use dark text on a light background.
Simple is best – probably black on white.

Large coloured headline to gain attention.
Red is best particularly if the rest is low-key.

Use left-aligned text with a plain easy to read font.
Arial or Verdana are good.

Emphasize important stuff with bold or italic type.
Prospect won't read every word **BUT** they will read these ones.
Make sure facts, features, benefits stand out.

Break longer passages of text with sub-headings.
They can blend together otherwise.

Set key points and features with bullet points.
This is easy.
Check your spelling.
Unless you intend to feature bad spelling use the spell-check.

7. Payment and shipping

You must receive payment BEFORE you ship anything.
Shipping can be hard enough.
But getting your painting back is considerably more difficult.

PayPal is encouraged by eBay.
There are so many advantages that you should offer this service.
You will be able to accept credit card payments as well.
Cheques, money orders and bank transfers are expensive time consuming.
The **BIG** advantage is that it is global – you can get paid from anywhere.
At least 75% of eBay clients prefer to use PayPal.
You will need a Premier or Business account.

How to use PayPal preferred.
On your Account Overview page click Profile tab.
Under Selling Preferences click Auctions.
On the Auction Accounts page under PayPal Preferred on eBay click On/Off.
When turned **ON** a PayPal message is inserted in the eBay View Item page.
AND the eBay Choose Payment Method page of **ALL** your listings.

Sign up for a PayPal Preferred account.
https://www.paypal.com/cgi-bin/webscr?cmd=xpt/auctions/PaypalPreferred-outside.
You now get 1% cash back on all PayPal ATM/debit cards.

Accepting credit cards helps overcome buyer inhibition.
Use PayPal's secure processing service.
You can upgrade a PayPal Personal account to accept credit card payments.

Dealing with non-payers.
Automatically notify winning bidder of shipping and handling charges.
Also tell them of your preferences for payment.
No payment after successive requests notify eBay and relist auction.
There will be no charge for the relisting.
If a non-payer leaves negative feedback ask eBay to remove it.

Make sure your work arrives by creating a shipping plan.
Let people know when you have sent the painting.
Here are some points to cover.

Once people buy they want their stuff – straight away.
So delivery **SPEED** is a priority.

Have a system that guarantees careful packaging.
Use the same system and improve it.

Inexpensive freight - keep in line with your competitors.
Shop around for best price.
Overseas freight can be more expensive.
Make sure you know whether tax and duty is payable – if so how much.
Many freight companies provide tracking numbers.
Pass this information on to the buyer.
Is tracking an extra charge – sometimes it is.
Save on shipping!
Anticipate buyer questions so provide all the information you can.
Tell the client which carrier, and what it will cost.

Save money on packaging.
Get all the free stuff you can from your postal service or carrier.
Buy anything else on eBay as cheaply as possible.
Buy in bulk to reduce costs.
Use recycled materials if they are in good condition.
Freight multiple works to the same buyer in one package.

Make sure your stuff arrives in top condition.
Corrugated cardboard is better than flat sheet.
Use foam or bubble plastic to wrap around your framed work.
Can you drop the package on the ground without anything breaking?
Make sure you use packaging tape in double quantities.
Secure any label with a layer of clear tape.
Don't use newspaper to wrap anything with.
The ink comes off and it flattens during transit.
Don't use anything that will move during transit.
Writing fragile makes **NO** difference **BUT** good wrapping does.

Have a special area where wrapping materials are stored ready to use.
Have postal scales so accurate estimate of weight and cost of shipping.
Make sure the scale can weigh what you send after packing.
Create a freight assembly line in your studio.
Set things up in the order you will use them.
If space line up paintings according to the auction stage they have reached.
Setting up this system takes time **BUT** when you have it then time is saved.

Print labels for your package and save time and money.
Depending where you live you may be able to print shipping labels online.
EBay offer this service through PayPal.

Print two labels and put one inside the package and the other outside.
Print as much information as possible BUT only ship to verified addresses.

Use the right freight company to deliver economically and on time.
Register courier and mailing services who deliver domestically and overseas.
Don't forget the post office.

Postage tip from Mike Barr – Adelaide, Australia.
Always send by registered mail.
Some items may be too big to send via post - couriers are then needed.
In Australia, Pack and Send are very good at sending art.
Get an idea of the cost to send so you can alert buyers before bidding.

Use promotional flyers to bring clients back.
Put promotional flyers in your shipping package.
Then one-time buyers can be enticed to become repeat buyers.
For example thank them and ask to be placed on their Favorite Sellers list.
Then eBay will mail them weekly updates of **YOUR NEW** auction listings.
You'll also get their email address.
Now you can contact them direct and build your relationship.

Don't forget your name, eBay Seller ID, and the URL of your website.
Keep your flyer to a maximum of one double sided page in length.
Any longer and people are likely to skip reading it.

A thank you lets the client know you appreciate their business.
Congratulations on purchasing a painting by Joe Bloggs (that's you).
This extends the feeling of excitement the client gets by winning the auction.
This also reduces buyer regret and thus cuts your refund rate.

A short biography and photograph shows a real person behind listing.
This makes things more personal and helps build a connection.

If you like this painting by Joe Bloggs (you again).
Now suggest another work you have for sale related to the original sale.
Include a brief description, an image, and the details of the listing.
What you want is for them to check it out.
Also remind your client about adding you to their Favorite Sellers page.

Offer limited time discount on next purchase for a sense of urgency.
If this is a first purchase you want them to buy more and be regular clients.
A discount can move an item that has not otherwise attracted attention.
Ask for a five-star DSR feedback which is more likely if you ask politely.

4. MAKE 'REAL' MONEY!

Reviewed by Peter Schleiker – (Big Pine, California)
1. Selling junk on eBay is never going to make you rich!
2. Marketing is important.
3. What is sales copy in eBay?
4. Writing sales literature
5. Let's re-visit what a client is worth.

1. Selling "junk" on eBay is never going to make you rich.

The secret to eBay is key research tools for a steady, reliable income.
For example squeeze maximum value out of your 55 title characters
Titles for eBay listings convey a **LOT** of useful information in very little space.

55 characters is all the space you have in your title.

The line above this one has 55 characters.
That's all you've got to work with so every single characters has to count!
Eliminate all non-essential or distracting words.
Each character in a listing has one purpose, draw targeted traffic to listing.
Waste characters on words that don't do this your title won't be as effective.

Compare:
Oil Painting Framed From Artist Landscape Size 24x36
with:
L@@K!!!! GR8 DEAL!!!! Oil Painting!!!!

The first listing:
Maximizes the effectiveness of the 55 title characters.
Uses words a potential buyer would use to search for the item they need.
Types "oil painting," "Framed," "From Artist," "Landscape" or "Size 24x36"
This listing title will appear in the search results.

The second listing aims to attract attention.
Invisible to buyers performing searches on any term except "Oil Painting"!
No-one searches terms such as, "L@@K!!!!" or "GR8 DEAL!!!!"?

Include synonyms and spelling variations of your top keywords.
Not every item goes by a single common name.
What different ways your potential buyers might spell or describe a work?
Nude, portrait, figure... all could be used to describe the same work.
Include common spellings and descriptive terms people might use in a title.

Use eBay shorthand to free up more space in your title.
eBay acronyms free up characters for keywords that can't be shortened.
Such as the item type, brand, or size.
eBay has a complete list of acronyms.

Place your strongest keywords at the beginning of your title.
They're keywords people search most - make sure they see them in a title!
It's not enough to fill your title with searchable keywords and acronyms.
Think about how your title looks, and how people will read it on their screens.

Capitalize the First Letter of Each Word.
For ease of reading, capitalize the first letter of each word in your title.
Type every character in lower case keywords will blend into the search list.
That makes them harder to pick out.

Examples of keyword-rich titles that don't use unnecessary words:
Original Landscape Oil Painting, Warm Tones, 36'x24"
Oil Painting, Award Winning Artist, Local, Old Bridge, New
Pastel Garden Flowers Framed Last Century
Water Colour Color Seascape Peaceful Blue Variations Never Exhibited

But you should experiment to find the best key words for your work.

2. Marketing is important.

Most artists neglect this important element of their professional career.
But the successful ones don't!

Marketing is about creating the demand that leads to sales.
If you do the marketing right, then sales follow, almost automatically.
Marketing can be done quite cheaply, but it does take a commitment of time.
Time needs to be spent regularly on marketing activities and follow up as too.
Any artist can do most of the things suggested here.
They are basic strategies that can pay off with an increase in sales.

One way is to create alliances by doing some things free.
For example donate a painting to a local charity or large organization.
Give away works that have not sold (but still up to your usual standard).
Give word of mouth referrals a discount or gift when they make a purchase.
The discount could be a cheque made to a charity or large organization!
When the cheque is taken to the organization you are re-promoted to them.
If there are no sales there is no cost other than the original donation.

Participate in expos, art shows, art and craft fairs, or home fairs.
Wherever you think might be a place where you can find likely buyers.
In particular look for places where many people pass in only a few days.
Make sure your work becomes well known to all who view your site.

Visitors complete a form to win a painting, drawing, print, art tuition.
The form has information for your database as it was created to do that.
It will also obtain permission to contact the visitors from time to time.
From this database you conduct a direct mail campaign for expo visitors.
Invite them to your studio or gallery, tell about your latest work, what you like.
Offer a service the client might appreciate.
Free delivery, guarantee satisfaction, or reframe work to suit client's taste.
Things like this build rapport and a relationship by making clients feel special.
Send one of your cards on their birthday.

Join organizations so you can network with the people who belong.
Service clubs, sporting bodies, business organizations and similar groups.
They are used by many people for networking purposes.
Usually you have an advantage as the only artist, so people seek you out!
You could even be a guest speaker to these sorts of groups.
Talk about your own experiences but in a way they might be interested in.
For a business group, talk about the business of being an artist, for example.

BUT plan your campaign, don't join to see what happens.
That approach seldom leads to any great benefit (for you).
Be aware of community needs and support them where possible.
A local house burnt down, people raise money for replacement.
Offer a painting for sale, raffled or auctioned, the money goes to the cause.

'Where did you hear of my art?' is a first question to ask a new client.
Write the answer down.
Keep a record of all the answers you can convert this information into figures.
Say 20% of new clients come as a result of community needs projects.
Tracking new sales this way you are able to see what is working best for you.

When you win awards make sure they are given maximum publicity.
It should be publicized by whoever makes the award.
But you can leverage the effect.
Promote this on your letterhead.
Send photocopies from the paper announcing your win (you have written it).
Have blow-up copies displayed in your studio or gallery, and so on.
Make marketing a long term investment and sales will increase.
Plan your marketing strategies for the next 12 months.
Which means you can actually do them and see what the effect is.

Let's say you are going to approach a gallery.
Galleries basically sell artworks, most often paintings.
I repeat, galleries are there to sell.
If they do not sell they go out of business.
Even if they do sell they can still go out of business.
If their sales are not profitable.
So you can see a gallery is just like any other regular business.
You should not think of them any other way.

A gallery does not exist to do favours for poor struggling artists.
Neither does a gallery exist so any artist has a place to show his/her work.
A gallery exhibits works of an artist, it's because it's an effective way to sell.
A gallery shows a struggling artist, it's because they believe sales are there.
Perhaps now or possibly in the medium term.
You are seeking a business relationship with a gallery.
The objective is the exchange of money that follows a sale.

There are three ways a business that sells, can acquire stock.
Manufacture it themselves.
Purchase it from a manufacturer.
Hold the work on consignment, paying the manufacturer after the sale.

You are the manufacturer of your artworks.
It thus follows that you can sell them yourself.
This could be at a retail level, direct to the client (from your studio or gallery).
You can also sell on a wholesale to someone who will sell at the retail level.

In this case the wholesale price must be less than the retail price.
The retailer to make money must sell at a higher price (retail).
The retailer is also bearing the risk (high for art) that the work will not sell.
In slow moving retail areas the mark-ups are large in order to compensate.
Jewellery can be 150% or even more.
Quick selling lines (like food) may only have a mark-up of a few percent.
This means if you wish to sell direct to a gallery:
Your price must be such that they make money when they sell to a client.

You may also have your work on consignment and be paid after a sale.
This approach eliminates the risk factor for the gallery.
That means you bear the cost of the work not selling.
There are more works available than buyers to buy.
That creates the slow moving nature of art sales,
So consignment selling is quite common.
As it is in real estate for the same reasons.

But even there the retail seller still has to make money.
The amount earned from a sale on consignment is called a commission.
There is no commission earned unless there is a sale.
The amount they make must compensate for other purchases not sold.

Let's clarify with an example - Joe Bloggs sells from his studio gallery.
The price for each work varies but let's call it $A for artist's price.
If sold on consignment the wholesale price is $A − c (c = commission).
Gallery or dealer buys to resell the wholesale price is $A −c − rf (risk factor).

Joe has a work which he believes to be worth $1000.
Wholesale payment from consignment sale $600 ($400 or 40% commission).
On a direct wholesale sale (not easy to do) Joe might receive $300 or $400.
Perhaps he can negotiate more?
These sorts of figures are the reality of the business world

What is the least you'd accept for a painting in each situation?
Now you know what the score is and can plan accordingly.
But before dealing with galleries let's look at eBay.
eBay you can learn a great deal about selling without gallery involvement.
Selling is not based on guesswork but research.

3. What is sales copy in eBay?

Sales copy is all a reader needs to see the value of what you sell.
It answers the question: What's in it for me?
It is informative, entertaining, tells what is needed to know, and easy to read.

Sales copy guides prospects through key stages of the sales process.
It's a written version of a **GOOD** sale-person.
Sequenced steps generate excitement, address objections, and reassure.
This is easier to do with long copy than in a short paragraph.

Writing sales copy is a science which can be developed.
Short brief copy is OK for cheap stuff.
But you are starting to learn how to sell your stuff when it is expensive.
That's why you should use longer copy in your listings.
It takes some time to create good sales copy.
That's why you are starting now.

You do not need to write like an author or an academic.
Your personality will **ADD** to the effectiveness of your copy.
If you can't spell leave the spell-check alone and be the artist who can't spell.
You'll stand out and people will remember you for they buy from real people.
BUT it **IS** important to know something about the people you are writing to.

Start by using Advanced Search on the completed listings.
Look at the final sale price of other items like yours.
Look for auctions with the highest selling price and the most bids.
Check their product description.
Look for lowest number of bids and selling prices.
Assess if a product description may have discouraged people from bidding.
Look for lots of bids **BUT** lower selling price.
Was there anything that may have reduced the value in the eyes of a bidder?

Potential bidders are not all the same.
An expert on what you sell – a collector wants more detail, resists hype.
May pay more and is a serious buyer whose expectations you need to meet.

A researcher is wary about buying from eBay.
You need to answer every question and earn their trust.

Impulse buyers needs convincing the opportunity is too good to miss.
A bargain hunter wants quality at low price but their bids help drive price up.

An anxious new eBay buyer needs re-assurance about your honesty.
Generally more bids = higher prices.

Your description is NOT a description.
It's a selling tool.
It's the entire sales process.
It is your sales literature or copy.

Your copy should position your painting as unique and desirable.
It's actually the benefits for the buyer, which needs to be unique.
They also must set it apart from other paintings.

So what does your stuff do better or differently from others?
Are there special or unique features?
Will you add value by offering free bonuses?
Can you bundle your work with other stuff?
The key is to find **ONE** thing the opposition doesn't have.

Your headline is EXTREMELY important.
Make people stop for a closer look.
Create a problem your potential client can identify with.
Stress the main benefit from a solution to that problem.
Generate a desire to find out more **BUT** include the main keywords.

ALL buyers are seeking to solve a problem.
No problem = No buy.
Ask questions to identify with the prospect.
Get people thinking along the lines you want them to!

Identify with the prospect.
You are on their side helping them solve a problem.
Respond to your questions in a similar manner that they would.

Tell a story around the painting to add some interest.
This doesn't have to be the story **OF** the painting.
They need a story they tell their friends, which brings a smile to their face.

Provide an overview of your solution.
Just explain how your work can improve their life.
Why buy from an expensive gallery when you can get original art-work here.
Show the value of your offer as a solution to their problem.
Shows how purchasing will benefit them (the buyer).
What you write should have your personality.

Now describe more details.
This doesn't necessarily mean a description of the painting.
Describe the mat-board, frame, and packaging details.
What will a buyer actually get?
What makes this work stand out from others?
Your photographs are part of the description.

Answers any questions a reader might have.
For standard sized paintings you could have readymade frames.
Where could it be hung, also suggest multiples.
Invite more questions.

Provide compelling reasons to buy.
How does this work solve a problem for the prospect?
Actually translate each feature into a benefit for the buyer.
Tell the prospect exactly how their problem will be solved.

Assure readers of your credibility and integrity.
The more expensive your work the more important this is.
Generally in our field credibility is essential.
That means you should make sure they know they are buying from the artist.

There are other ways to build credibility too.
Provide some detail of your experience relevant to the work being sold.
Insert this information in your About Me page and you're My World page.
Make sure you are honest in all you do – describe your painting accurately.
Use testimonials from satisfied clients.
Paste some of your positive feedback into your auction listing.
Provide a link to your Feedback page – click here to view ALL my feedback.

Use correct spelling and grammar BUT sound friendly and informal.

One or more bonus helps people take that last step and bid.
The higher price your work is the more likely it is you would use this strategy.

Each bonus (free) increases the value (but not price) of a work for sale.
Every single thing that comes with the work should be listed as a bonus.
Mat-board, no glass, frame, hanging wire, special packaging, all bonus.

They do not have to be expensive but a bonus should be free.
Your biography might be a bonus in some cases – with a link to your website.
Create an eBook as a bonus – hanging your artwork – with a link to website.
Just send a link to the winning bidder so they can claim their bonus.

Make sure any terms and conditions are clear.
Provide purchasing instructions.
What are your payment options?
You can block buyers who don't have PayPal for example.

State when you will send the item (3 days after payment).
It's packed and ready to go – tell how much it weighs.
You send an email with details of total payment as soon as the auction ends.
Send email saying the painting has been sent as soon as it has.

Provide your shipping information.
Use eBay's Shipping Calculator – go to http://sell.ebay.com/sell.
Then Shipping and click Calculated.
Is there any tax or duty payable?
Provide contact details – your email address.
Don't go overboard with restrictions though.

Reassure bidders by providing a guarantee.
What is your returns policy?
Not satisfied - then send it back for a full refund.
Do **NOT** have a time limit for the warranty.
Ask them to contact you if not 100% satisfied – before any feedback.

Create urgency to encourage immediate bids.
People tend to put things off.
End your product description by telling about the benefits of ownership.
Emphasize the uniqueness.

Ask for the sale (well bid).
If they reach this point asking for the sale is quite natural.
So – ask for it.
Tell the prospect exactly what to do next.
Restate the main benefits from owning your painting.
Then – Place your bid now!

Don't forget the PS.
This is the next most read part of your sales copy after the headline.
It is a last chance to get a bid.

Restate your offer.
Repeat key benefits.

Emphasize prospect needs to take action NOW.
State what they will miss if they don't take immediate action.
Remind them that this is an ideal solution to their problem.

4. Writing sales literature

Is there a secret to selling successfully in writing?
You have to find the right words for the job!
If words don't grab visitors and keep them with your promotion, they leave.
Most visitors to whatever you have written take 10 seconds or less to decide.
That's all the time to convince them what you wrote is where they should be.
It doesn't matter how great your works are, or anything else.

The most important words are the ones in your headline!
Quite obviously your headline is the first thing your readers see.
It needs to capture attention, spark curiosity and compel them to read further.
The headline words also have to do all this **FAST**.

So what can you do?
Most readers are looking for information.
But that doesn't necessarily mean you should provide information.

They want information in relation to a problem they are trying to solve.
Perhaps they want contemporary coloured paintings for a rumpus room?
They could be trying to work out how to reframe a painting they've inherited?

Probably you don't know what the problem is they want to solve.
So you need to find out what their problem is and then relate to that.
You can do this verbally by questioning.
You can also ask questions in writing.

Alternatively what sorts of problems does your art solve?
If this demonstrates a genuine understanding of their wants and needs.
They'll be interested in what you have to say.
If it doesn't they were unlikely to buy anyway!

So present a solution to that problem.
You've described a problem, but now you have to solve it with your artwork.
You do this in a way that creates a powerful image in the mind of readers.
Get them to imagine the result and you're halfway down the track to a sale.
"How to…", "Discover…" headlines that help people imagine an end result.

Focus on benefits NOT features.
People aren't interested in descriptions of a painting or service (class).
But what it will do for them.
This isn't easy for an artist to do.
We don't usually think that way.

The important question in your reader's mind is "What's in it for ME?"
Make sure you answer this question.
Avoid telling and describing.

Don't tell them how great your art is.
Get them to see how great their life will be after hanging your work on a wall.
Any painting will do many different types of things for a variety of clients.

They imagine nods, smiles and admiring glances the new painting gets.
Every time someone sees it on their wall.
Imagine relief they feel when back in their wife or girlfriend's good books.

Write directly to your readers.
Write those headlines as if you are talking to your best client.
They are someone you know very well.
Make that person the focus of everything you write.

Write in the same way you speak.
You may need to modify this so you use the same language as your readers.
Your works appeal to leather clad bikers.
Do you write the same when addressing someone specializing in quilting?
If clients say "dude" then so do you, but if its "folks" then "dude" won't wash.

Make your headlines stand out.
Formatting is just as important as what you write.
Do you put words together with lots of commas, adverbs and adjectives?
Then pile one idea on another (even with comments in brackets).
It gets hard to remember how the sentence even began.
Definitely not the way to go, particularly for a headline.
Your headline can have a massive effect on your sales.
Spend quite a deal of time on it.
Help your readers get the meaning in a single glance.
Limit yourself to one important idea per line (I'm getting better).
Also use simple formatting such as bold and italics.

Once you have written a few headlines, TEST THEM.
See which works best- just play around with them and test again.
You may do this a few times before you discover one that works best.
It will be worth the effort.

Headlines and graphics are important.
They are used to attract attention and draw people into the rest of your story.
Headlines and graphics can also be used to qualify the readers.

This means they attract the attention of the RIGHT reader.
You paint local landscapes.
It doesn't matter if art lovers interested in abstracts, don't read what you say.
They're unlikely to be your buyers anyway.

A great deal of thought should be put into the heading and graphics.
Most people do not put enough time into this aspect.
They miss attracting people who would be interested in what they say or sell.
Now you need to build interest and desire (for your works).
A copywriter's approach is to sell the benefits of owning your artwork.
To do this you need to focus on what's in it for the buyer.
Why will they be better off owning one of your paintings?

Some ideas that will help your copy include
Write the way you speak, then people will read as if you are talking to them.
It's more personal too because your character is conveyed.
Avoid complicated words and jargon unless they're what readers use.
As well as having pictures, use your words to build pictures.
Then your client can easily imagine whatever it is you are referring to.

It is better to understate than exaggerate.
Reduce exaggeration by using fewer adjectives.
As well as being truthful what you say should be believable.

Use sub-headings and bullet points.
Break your heading up and make your copy easy to read
Repeat key words and phrases to emphasize main points.
Then people are likely to remember these points too.

The last paragraph or back page is your final chance.
Don't waste this space for it may actually be the first thing your reader sees.
That's why it's often a good place to restate your offer.
A 'PS' is also a critical area.
People often look at this without reading anything else!
Finally make sure your contact details are clearly displayed.

List reasons why people might be better off buying your paintings.
Cross out ones of benefit for you, the reasons left can be in your copy.

Use ordinary language
Headings, sub-headings, indentations, etc are the main part of your writing.
They should attract people interested in what you're writing about.
That is what your works can do for them.

A heading must attract attention, so you might indent or make it BOLD.
Base the heading and the content, on a WIIFM (What's In It For Me).
Your name in the heading will appeal to people who know you.
Thus the heading has qualified (sorted out) the likely clients for your work.
But this will not attract people who don't know you, will it?

You must identify your work in some other way to attract these people.
You should consider different copy for different kinds of clients or prospects!
What you write for someone who collects your work?
That will be different from someone who shows interest, but hasn't bought.
What about those who bought other artists but not shown interest in you?
Obviously they are not familiar with your work, and may not be interested.
You need to sort out which group someone belongs to.
Some people know how you do things but others will not.

What purpose does your copy have?
Assume the reader is interested and therefore will want to buy.
Use teaser information and questions, to move the reader to the next step.
Tell a client what they need to know as your aim is they eventually buy.
Many will not be interested – but don't worry about them at all.

Focus more on the value factors.
That's this artist (yourself) rather than any special price.
Well, what are they and how do you do this?
What people know about, you don't need to stress.

Value builders must be specific.
WIIFM does not have to be stated by you, but correctly inferred by reader.
They say 'Which means that ....'

Allude to the benefit for the buyer rather than actually stating it.
Give facts and figures.
This teaser and questions keep the prospect moving towards a purchase.

Here are some examples of value builders and an inferred WIIFM:
VB-popularity
WIIFM-belong to group, security, impress others, reassurance, has status
VB-Sales record (numbers sold, $ sold, average $ sold)
WIIFM-status, impress others, save money, feel secure.
VB-Status
WIIFM-others envy, investment, feel secure, belong to group, improve self.
VB-How works help
WIIFM-decoration, status, impress others, pleasure.

VB-Decoration
WIIFM-impress others, pleasure, status
VB-Colour
WIIFM-use as decoration, fashion, reward self, pleasure, belong.
VB-Skill
WIIFM-Others admire, envy, pleasure, improve self, status
VB-Subject (local/wildlife)
WIIFM-gain pleasure, belong to group, security
VB-Others who have bought artist, illustrious buyers,
WIIFM-feel secure, belong, status
VB-Testimonials
WIIFM-feel secure, status, impresses others
VB-Exhibition record (how many, where at)
WIIFM-investment potential, envy, status, security
VB-Price rises
WIIFM-investment, buy now, save money, security
VB-Awards won
WIIFM-security, status, impress others
VB-Positions held
WIIFM-security, status
VB-Limited availability, rarity,
WIIFM-save money, status
VB-Style,
WIIFM-pleasure, impresses others, belong to group
VB-Beauty,
WIIFM-pleasure, security, improve self
VB-Timelessness,
WIIFM-save money, security
VB-Creativity,
WIIFM-pleasure, improve self
VB-Student of, or other associated artists,
WIIFM-status, security
VB-Nostalgia
WIIFM-feeling secure, impresses others, pleasure, belong to group)

Instead of writing that your art is a great investment.

Make sure a reader discovers how your prices have risen in recent years.
From $x to $x5.
Those interested in appreciation your artworks will get the message.
So will some others.

State your offer, assuming the reader is interested.

Remember to stress **VALUE FACTORS**.

Make sure the prospect knows what to do.
Walk through the purchase steps with them.
You must have a 'Call for Action' or there's a risk nothing actually happens.
For example: Phone 2222 5555 for an appointment.

5. What a client is worth.

Many might be worth a great deal of money.
Unless some of that comes your way it makes no difference to how you live.
So the question really is how much is a client worth to **YOU.**

How often do people buy?
People buy petrol almost daily and most smokers buy almost daily too.
On the other hand most people don't buy a house anywhere near as often.

Well how often do people buy your artworks?
Do you know?
Can you guess?

How much do you make on each sale?
For many sales a gallery's commission is deducted from the sale price.
The frame is also a deduction.
What else has to be considered?
The cost of attracting a client is one factor (often part of gallery commission).

Usually it costs less for later transactions that the initial one.
Then it's not a matter of building interest but tapping the interest that's there.
Fame is a good illustration of this phenomenon.

It's possible to work out how much to spend attracting a new client.
If we have this kind of information,
Then we pay agents, sales people, galleries, advertising accordingly.
What if a sales-person gets **ALL** profit on a **FIRST SALE** to a **NEW** buyer?
Offer a first sale discount where your entire margin goes to the salesperson.
Provided the profit on future sales is sufficient.

Here's how you can calculate the long-term value of a client.
The $ cost per client to get (obtain, capture) them = **A**.
The $ return per sale = **B**.
The number of purchases by a client in a year (average) = **C**.
The buying life of a client in years = **D**.

The life-time value of a client = (B x C x D) – A
If **C** and **D** are sufficient, it's possible to make little or nothing on the first sale.
Yet make a great deal in the long run.
Consider special deals mobile phone companies offer to join their system.
Those deals are built on this aspect of business.

For example a typical client might cost $450 to obtain.
Your average return per sale is $900.
People buy 1½ works in a year on average.
A buyer keeps buying for 5 years before 'their walls are full'.
These are made up figures just to illustrate the long-term value of a client.

In this case the long-term value is $6,300.
Does this give you a different perspective?

You need to keep the necessary figures for a period of time.
Then these calculations become reasonably accurate guides.
Initially you guess but that is better than not doing this kind of thinking at all!
Most artists have a transactional view of sales, they think in single units.
This does not provide you with the full picture (so to speak).

Using a similar approach calculate the $ per enquiry and $ per sale.
Then determine the effectiveness of your advertising and other promotions.

Maintain and develop a relationship with each client with a contact list.
That can continue over the years needed for long-term value to be realized.
Your first-time clients always cost you the most.
Instead of spending time, money, and energy finding more first-time visitors.
Devote more time to relationships you establish with your current client base!

Never-the-less, new clients are obviously very important.
Even though they probably cost you quite a deal to obtain.
Your aim should be to turn them into ongoing loyal clients!
Then they can replace existing clients who cease buying.
You also develop your client base so your income stream increases.

A good start is to send a personal letter, in ten days of first purchase.
If you have so many clients this presents a problem, you are ahead.
Mostly you'll be able to find the time to write the letters.

Your letter can thank them in a way that adds to yourself as an artist.
Also enhance the organization that made the sale on your behalf.
Generally this can be done by asking questions.

In your letter you can also re-sell your value.
This doesn't mean boast about your achievements!
Instead mention again the factors that led to the client making the purchase.
If the work was for a particular place in their home - so ask how it looks.

Re-sell the prudence of the purchase so they've made a wise decision.
Did someone else want to buy the work just after they'd made their choice?

If you made the sale possibly you could offer of an additional product.
That might be a box of cards, a print, or service (free valuations).
You might also mention your guarantee, next exhibition, etc.
You might also consider each of these as the subject for follow-up letters.

The main point of your letter is to reinforce the buyer's decision.
Tell the new client you will personally be in touch from time to time.
Tell them different things or let them know something or ask for their opinion.
An aspect of this is, around Christmas time, send a letter rather than card.
They are cheaper and better.
They're perceived as more personal and an example of awesome service.

Don't worry about mailing new clients too often – or anyone too often.
Tests showed that from one mailing $x sales resulted for a particular product.
From a second mailing, done almost straight away $x + 50% sales resulted.

An even better result is when a mailing is followed by a phone call.
Here sales in the above experiment resulted in $x + 60% to 1000%.
It's a good idea to telephone people after a mailing - ask if they got the letter.
Your aim is to press a hot-button.
So test your tests by telephoning to seek reactions to the letter.

Here's an experiment.
Send a letter that requires a response.
Re-mail to those who don't respond and see what the difference is.
You could also mail to everyone again.
See what difference there is between initial responders and those who didn't.

5. WRAPPING UP.

Reviewed by: Gilles Durand – (Crolles, France)
1. Consider an eBay store.
2. An eBay store is THE BEST way to get exposure on eBay.
3. Use advanced tools once your store is established.
4. How does your store appear to prospects?
5. Build a contact list.
6. Why should you automate?
7. Become a Top Rated Seller
8. Introduce your art to whole new audiences on eBay?

1. Consider an eBay store.

A store can increase sales, profit margins, and total revenue.
If your store stands out, is personalized it separates you from a hobby seller.
Start with a Basic Store at $15.95 a month.

You get an internet address (URL).
Link other things to this (website, blog) and drive traffic to your eBay stuff.
There's no need for constant updating either.
Show **ALL** you have for sale if you want and still run regular auctions too.

Lower selling costs.
Store listings cost 3c a month with Gallery image.
Look at http://pages.ebay.com/help/sell/storefees.html

You can get sales reports and traffic reports.
They tell the keywords buyers use to find your store, pages they view, etc.
There is accounting assistance too and it is possible to link with QuickBooks.

A Help Line is available.
Phone support is provided.

There are sales management tools too.
Selling Manager (Basic, Pro, Featured and Anchor) save time, improve client satisfaction.

EBay's fee structure assists professional store owners!
EBay promotes this as their "lowest insertion fees ever!"
Auctions with a starting price of less than $1, insertion fees are waived.
Backend fees for auctions are higher.

When you sell an item via auction (and don't operate an eBay Store).
You pay 8.75% for the first $25 of final price, and 3.5% for the rest to $1000.
A store you pay a flat 9% on the total price of the auction, to $50 maximum.
This is great if you sell big-ticket items costing over $1000.
BUT if you sell items that are less, you pay a **LOT** more in Final Value Fees.
Here's an example to illustrate:
You list an auction for one of your oil paintings, and the winning bid is $200.
Previously you paid 8.75% of the first $25 you make, and 3.5% of the $175.
Your total Final Value Fee was $2.19 + $6.13 = $8.32.
Now the same painting for the same price.
The Final Value Fee is $18.00.
That's quite a difference!

There is a benefit for store owners.
In contrast, Final Value Fees for eBay Store owners is largely unchanged.
Store owners can add to 12 photos to each listing **FREE** bonus save money.
EBay also puts regular Store listings into their search results.
That gives search exposure equal to auction and regular "Buy It Now" listing!

EBay rewards professional eBay Store owners.
EBay is forcing small timers to up their game and go professional.
Otherwise it just doesn't make sense to do business on eBay.
Unless you're selling big-ticket items for they're simply not worth your while.
Except as a way of learning to sell – then it's cheap!
Be a full-time professional Store owner.

But there are some drawbacks to an eBay store.
A store doesn't get the same exposure as an auction in the search results.
BUT here **ARE** strategies you can use to overcome this.
Balance store and auction items.
Then you can cross-promote from one to the other.
Feature similar and identical items in both formats.
This doesn't have to be for all variations (size, colour, etc.).
Have at least one auction to direct traffic to the store for similar items.
Go to http://pages.ebay.com/help/sell/cp-setup.html

Promote you eBay store OFF eBay as much as possible.
Use the link regularly from website, emails, etc.
This saves 75% of the final fee value and is easy to do.

Use keywords in your store listings.
This will help buyers find items.
It will also help bring bidders searching complete eBay listings.

2. An eBay store is THE BEST way to get exposure on eBay.

Your store has two goals.
It should drive more traffic to your listings.
It should save you money in listing fees.
More exposure means more sales.
It is easier to get and keep repeat clients with a store.

An eBay store is basically like a website.
There are many ways to customize an eBay Store.
Make sure you have a good name – use searchable keywords for a start.
Start customizing your store.
Click the Store icon (a little door) or type the URL into your web browser.
Click the link Seller, Manage Store near the bottom right of your store page.
Bookmark this page for future access.

Logo
Don't pay anything until you have a design you **LOVE**.

Store description:
Try to use all the allowed characters.
Use searchable keywords for this is how searchers find your store.

Templates and themes:
Have a look, choose the best for your art business - you might do your own.

Store header:
Your store header should have some description with keywords.

Item display:
View your store using List View and Gallery View, decide which you like best.
You can change what your prospects see when they first enter your store.

Store categories:
Create all the categories you think you might ever need.
Use keywords that make sense to your prospects to create those categories.
You can put them into any order you want and change it too.
It will not matter if there is nothing in a category.
Only categories containing listings are shown to buyers.

Promotion boxes:
Create some boxes you can put around your store to promote items.
Promote your newsletter, specials, or anything else.

Listing header:
This shows up on **ALL** your listings.
It can promote your store, display your logo, sell your newsletter, etc.

Search engine keywords:
EBay pulls these from your listings in each category.
Monitor them and make changes to keywords that work best (after testing).

Listing feeds:
Turn **BOTH** of these **ON** to get more **OFF** eBay exposure.

Cross promotion:
Update cross-promotion preferences to get more exposure.
Make changes and test some of the options.

Selling managers:
Subscribe (free) to gain more control.

Custom pages:
Create additional store pages **AND** highlight specific items.

Create a Store Policies page.
Promote specials **AND** whatever you like that eBay allows.

HTML builder.
Create links to sites or pages not on your store with Referral Code save fees.

3. Use advanced tools once your store is established.

You continue to grow your store as long as you supply the artworks.
There are many more tools available now.

Traffic and sales reports:
More information about your prospects and clients.

Send emailed promotions.
Send to those who ask for your newsletter and mark you as a favourite seller.
Create a paper flyer to include with shipments.
Thank your clients and promote your store and other works.

Get a Seller Outreach review.
Seller Outreach: eBay personally reviews your store and listings with you.
They help with actionable suggestions on increasing your effectiveness.
Go to sellergrowth@ebay.com they will call you and send follow up emails.

Visit the eBay Stores Discussion Board.
Find out stuff from other store owners.
Go to http://forums.ebay.com/db2/forum.jspa?forumID=21 .

Want a holiday?
There are options so prospects know you are temporarily unavailable.
Go to http://pages.ebay.com/help/specialtysites/placing-store-vacation.html

Upgrade your store.
Get more exposure and even more options.
You can get **BIGGER** just as long as you can supply the artworks.

Have a SALE with Markdown Manager.
Discount your works or shipping.
Display special offers when they are live.
Go to http://pages.ebay.com/storefronts/markdownmanager.html .

4. How does your store appear to prospects?

Open your store page and look for 10 sec without scrolling down.
Is it an appropriate store name with keywords?
Is there a call to action on your opt-in offers?
Can prospects add you to Favourites list and bookmark your store easily?
Does it make you want to stay and shop?
Is the page easy to read?
Is it an appealing layout?
Is the theme suitable for your image and artworks?
Is the page neat and organized?
Has the colour been well handles?
Does the list or gallery view suit the design?
Is the search box easy to find?
Does your logo look professional?
Are the custom categories keyword laden and well organized?
Are the Promo Boxes present and well-placed?
Can prospects sign up for a newsletter?
Are the RSS feeds turned on?

Now start making improvements.
Every step gets you closer to a top eBay business.

But what about the About Me page?
Here's where you can tell prospects more about yourself.
You can establish your credibility and build relationships with prospects.
It is a mini-website for marketing your eBay business.
You can provide links to your listings and store.
You can also collect opt-in addresses to build a contact list.

Why do YOU buy from sellers?
What do they do that makes you trust them?
Do they seem like a genuinely good person?
Do they make you feel welcomed and valued?
Do they know a lot about what they sell?
Are they experienced or have expertise in their field?
Do they answer questions in a clear and informative manner?
Do other people say good things about them?
Do they have clear payment information and a good guarantee?

Now do the same things for your clients!
Your About Me page is an opportunity to treat your prospect with respect.
Share helpful information.

A short biography:
A little bit about who you are and where you are from.
Be friendly and somewhat chatty.
Include such things as your participation in the art business,
The main purpose is to show you are reliable to buy from – nothing else.

Your business history on eBay:
Tell what you sell and how you started selling.
Talk about how your non-eBay experience brought you to eBay.
The reason is show expertise, knowledge and seriousness on doing it right.

Something about what you sell.
You want to show prospects you know your business and will share it.

Frequently asked questions:
A FAQ allows you to anticipate prospect questions and answer them upfront.
This shows the prospect you are well-informed and helpful.
It also saves answering the same questions repeatedly.

Recent feedback:
Including feedback shows you have feedback you are happy to share.
It also shows you value what your clients have to say about you.
Prospects are re-assured by recommendations from people like themselves.
The **BEST** feedback describes specific benefits of buying from you.

Include terms and conditions.
Clear these up for prospects.
It is the same, but possibly less detailed than, on auction listing page.
Be polite.

Promote your About Me page.
Every auction you list should have a link to your About Me page.
Make sure the About Me page also links back to each listing.

Use the About Me page to send prospects to your auctions or store.
Send visitors to your active listings.
Include a list of your current listings on your About Me page.
This gives people an easy way back to where they probably came from.
BUT they might find other items you have and go there instead.

Send visitors to your eBay store.
List items available in your store.

Cross-promote and up-sell to prospects already interested in your stuff.
Reasons why you should drive traffic to your store:
Buyers will search your store and not be diverted elsewhere.
You will save time and money.
Once your store is set up it is easier and cheaper than regular listings.
It looks more professional.
Your About Me is a mini-website.
AND your eBay Store is the e-commerce companion.

How you format your About Me page can make more sales.
Possible elements you could consider.
A short biography.
Details of your eBay business.
Your experience or expertise.
Keywords about your items to attract search engines and off-eBay prospects.
Pictures linked to your business.
Answers to frequently asked questions.
Recent feedback.
Terms and conditions.
Links to eBay listings, store, reviews, My World page and opt-in contact list.

Start creating your About Me page.
Go to http://pages.ebay.com/help/account/about-me.html
Click the Create About Me link.
Use the step-by-step option.

Spend time making your title as relevant as possible.
Make sure you attract search engines.
Your title needs to contain keywords for likely searches.

The paragraph content is VERY important.
Spend time making this information relevant and useful.
You can have more than two paragraphs if you use HTML paragraph tags.
Use keywords to make sure the content responds to searches.

You can add two images with labels.
This will probably be enough.

Feedback, listings and other pages:
Build your credibility by adding 5 to 10 feedback comments.
Display the maximum number of current listings allowed.
Link to other pages that are relevant to your artworks.

Select one of three layout designs.
You can change to another if you wish.
There is an **EDIT** link that lets you make changes easily and quickly.

The My World page also attracts prospects.
Make sure you use the right keywords.
Then you can send prospects to your listings, or store.

5. Build a contact list.

You CAN use an OPT-IN form on your About Me page.
You should collect at least first name, last name and email address.
With permission from the subscriber you can develop a relationship.

Market to these prospects again and again.
Send them any news – stuff that has happened.
You can generate repeat business - from people who have bought before.

OK what will you offer?
You need to attract interest and generate a reason to sigh-up.
A free newsletter subscription is common – but you have to write newsletters!
Just an article on hanging artworks might be enough.
A screensaver featuring one of your works is another idea.
Being able to participate in a survey could also work.
EVERY time you do an auction listing include a link to your About Me page.

Your About Me page check list - the 10 second test.
Read the content of your page and look at the headline.
Will prospects get a good idea of who you are and what you sell?
Can they easily see what the focus of your business is?

Are there one or more calls to action?
Ask your prospects to do something - even "Bid now!" will do.

Is the content relevant?
Is the content directly related to running your eBay business?
Does it create a professional impression?

Are there keywords in your headline and page content?
Search engines can drive prospects to your page from outside eBay.

Is there a re-assuring guarantee?
Can you help the prospect guard against them making a mistake?

Is there an FAQ section?
Save time answering the same questions.

Does the page include feedback comments?
More than anything else these provide you with credibility.

Is there payment information?
Your terms and conditions should be uncomplicated and easy to read.
They should be presented in a friendly and helpful manner.

Does your page have an opt-in form?
Build a list of loyal clients that you can contact regularly.

Are there links to your eBay Store and existing auctions?
Make it easy for them to find the stuff they can but.

Is your page positive and friendly?
Make sure prospects know you are easy to deal with.

Does it make prospects feel comfortable?
Is there an impression that doing business with you will be easy?
AND hassle-free?
Would they feel you are knowledgeable and trustworthy?

Is your expertise and experience highlighted?
Prospects should feel you know about what you sell.

Is there a logo and photo?
These features attract attention.

6. Why should you automate?

Instead of wasting time on repetitive tasks paint more works to sell.
Automation allows you to make real money without leaving eBay.
Automate **BEFORE** you have to.

Design professional looking auction listings.
You can obtain templates into which you insert your information.
Templates provide a consistent appearance for your listings.
This becomes a part of your brand.

List more auctions at the same time.
Just supply details of what is to be sold and when but do it all in advance.

Monitor your auctions.
There are tools to help you keep track of what happens.
They report to you in an easy to understand format.

Follow up automatically by email.
Keep prospects up to date about your auctions.
Respond to questions immediately.
Send thank-you emails.
Set up your feedback system.

Manage your financial affairs.
Budgets, shipping costs, auction fees all add up.
Many small financial items can become hard to track.

Manage auctions remotely.
New wireless technology means you can be anywhere.

Reduce your research time.
A range of tools can dramatically cut the amount of time **YOU** spend.
At the same time they can dramatically increase the information you receive.
Calculate shipping charges accurately and quickly.
Your charges will also be fair for your client.
Here are some eBay tools you can use.

Turbo Lister (http://pages.ebay.com/turbo_lister)
Free tool for creating multiple listings.
List items all at once, save listings and re-use them later.
Turbo Lister supplies templates to easily create listings.
Listings are easily and quickly scheduled and placed with this tool.

EBay Toolbar (http://pages.ebay.com/ebay_toolbar).
Gives alerts to My eBay, Announcements, the Community Hub, and PayPal.
You can view the top items you are selling.
The Account Guard lets you know if you view a genuine eBay page or a fake.

**Selling Manager
(http://pages.ebay.com/selling_manager/products.html):**
Access to email and feedback templates, bulk feedback processing, bulk re-listing, templates for invoices, downloadable sales history and other features.
There is a $4.99 a month fee.

Accounting Assistant (http://pages.ebay.com/accountingassistant):
Works with QuickBooks accounting program.
Exports eBay and PayPal data to QuickBooks.
Free for store owners and subscribers to Selling Manager.

Auctiva (www.auctiva.com).
Listing templates, image hosting, advanced editing features, sales tools, a store, checkout.
Bulk campaign scheduling, pre-filled item information, customizable automatic emailing, re-listing.

Irfanview graphics software (www.irfanview.com):
Simple to use image editing program.
Cheaper and easier to use than Photoshop.
Fix and polish your photos to make your images stand out.

7. Become a Top Rated Seller

Know how to optimize your listings for eBay Search.
For Top Rated Seller status; sell at least $3,000 a year over 100+ sales.
Listings appear near the top of eBay's searches so more people see them.

Write relevant, keyword-rich titles.
A good impression-to-click-through ratio, closer your listing is to top results.
Everyone sells Product X, but more click your listings than your competitors'.
Get 10 clicks and a competitor gets 2, your listing is higher in search listings.
Make sure your listing titles grab people's attention.
Encourage many people to click as possible.
How do you do this?
Make sure keywords people type into eBay's search engine is in your title.
People can immediately see you're offering exactly what they're looking for.
But you also have to make sure your title is **RELEVANT.**

Make sure your titles are UNIQUE.
You have to make sure your listing titles stand out in the search results.
Create unique, keyword-rich titles and subtitles that stand out from others.
Then compete against anyone!

Provide excellent service to keep your Detailed Seller Rating "clean".
In order to achieve Top-Rated Seller status, you need a 4.6 average DSR.
BUT you need **NO** more than two 1-star or 2-star ratings in any category.
That means you have to offer top-notch service to all your buyers.
If you deal with an unhappy buyer, do anything to resolve the situation
Get the low mark struck from your record.
Offer free shipping.
This ensures your listings are higher in eBay's 'Best Match" search results.
EBay gives a boost to listings that offer free shipping to their clients.
You get a better position in search results and major points with buyers!
Just be sure free shipping won't deep-six your profits!

Make sure your listings CONVERT.
EBay rewards proven seller listings by a boost in the search listings.
So how do you make sure your listing converts?
Follow recommended best practices to qualify for Top-Rated Seller status.
The requirements aren't hard to achieve, and they benefit buyers and sellers.
Small sellers with good communication with clients can compete.

Sellers who offer the best value see their listings sell more quickly.
Listings with better sales-copy and guarantees convert to sales efficiently.
Not to mention the 20% discount on your final value fees.

EBay Selling Manager is free!
Bulk-manage listings, send bulk feedback, print shipping labels and invoices.
There are add-on applications that are free to try for the first 30 days.
Then you check them out and see which ones would be most useful for you.
Selling Manager Pro, an upgrade costs $15.99 a month.
It offers automatic listing, buyer auto notification, and other useful options.
Try it free for 30 days, compare the two options and see which works best.
Automated software like Selling Manager or Selling Manager Pro save time.
Devote more of your time to growing a business instead of simply running it.
If you're always catching up, never able to check these software programs.

Market research is an important step to take building an eBay business.
Yet it's the one most eBay sellers ignore!
It's not enough for you to offer a quality product.
You also have to know the secrets of how to create magnetic eBay listings.
They compel people to make a bid or click on the "Buy it Now!" button.
In order to reach out to your prospects and beat your rivals.
You need to create a keyword-loaded title that stands out in search results.
Write compelling headlines that draw people into the rest of your listing.
You need to know simple sales-copy tricks that drive visitors to take action.
Whether it's making a bid or purchase or checking out your other auctions.
That's just the "sales-copy" part of your listing!

You must also know how to...
Get feedback ratings to establish credibility, overcome visitors' objections
Use photographs which drive up your final selling price
Choose the right category for eBay's ready-to-buy shoppers.
Implement payment and shipping strategies for money in a PayPal account
Test new techniques and track results - use the best in all auctions.

Automation is the beautiful part of running an eBay business.
With automation tools available you can set up a business to run hands-free.
You only need a few hours a week to manage campaigns **AND** grow profit!

Here's some automation tools that make life easier as an eBay seller:
Auctiva
eBay Accounting Assistant
eBay Blackthorne Basic
eBay Blackthorne Pro

eBay Solutions Directory
eBay TurboLister
Selling Manager Pro

Some automation tools are free or available to eBay store owners only.
Use the best automation opportunities from eBay -- you need an eBay store.
An eBay store makes listings more professional.
AND will increase credibility as a legitimate seller.
EBay's store owners have tools to build, manage, promote, track business.
These tools will help you get the edge on competitors -- especially if no store.

Once you reach this step, you should have your own eBay store.
NOW increase your business by promoting to the entire world!
Use proven "search engine optimization" strategies to turbo-charge listings.
They are at the top of search results for Google and major search engines.
Even create your own off-eBay website to capture more high-quality traffic.
Use your "About Me" page to build a list of potential buyers.
Contact via email to let them know about your new listings.

Sometimes "FREE" isn't all it's cracked up to be
EBay has a "5 Free Insertion Fees Every 30 Days" promotion.
Any starting price and **NO** Insertion Fees on first five auction-style listings.
Every month when you use eBay's "Sell Your Item" or "Simple" listing form.
If your items don't sell, you pay nothing.
Other auctions revert to a Insertion Fee and Current Value Fee system.
If five items sell, pay flat rate of 8.75% of final value OR $20 whichever lower.

Here's the math:
Say you auction a print starting at $9.99 and selling for $100...
List 5 Free system: $0.00 + $8.75 = $8.75.

But you can avoid paying these extra fees.
Your first five auctions are items that will sell for up to $25 or $500 or more.
These five "free" insertion fees don't work if you use automated software.
Could eBay's Turbolister or third-party tool like Auctiva to manage fuctions?
If auctions aren't under $25 or over $500 use software for every listing.

When to use List 5 Free

Final Value =	$0 - $25	$25.01 - $500	$500.01+	Automated listing
	OK	NO	OK	OK

To guarantee you don't spend more than needed on your listing fees.
Always calculate exactly what your final value fees will end up costing you.

Use a tool such as this eBay and PayPal Fee Calculator.
A few seconds research could save you a **LOT** of money in the long run.

8. Introduce your art to whole new audiences on eBay?

EBay is a really useful tool for promoting a normal Internet business.
But there is a right way to use eBay for promoting an off-eBay website.
AND a wrong way.
The right way can drive huge waves of qualified visitors to your business.
But the wrong way can get you banned from doing business on eBay again!

Here's what eBay's stringent regulations say you can't do:
DON'T include any links to your off-eBay website in your auction listings
DON'T include any links to your website in your eBay store or custom pages
DON'T include an opt-in offer in your auction listings
DON'T include an opt-in offer in your eBay store
DON'T automatically add clients or visitors to your auctions to your opt-in list
DON'T overtly try to send people off eBay.
DON'T collect information for marketing purposes.
On auction listings, eBay store, custom page without eBay's expressed consent.

Well, there is one place you can include a link to your off-eBay website.
AND you can put an opt-in form there to collect people's email addresses.
So you can build a relationship with them.
AND promote your products to them in the future.
You **CAN** use your "About Me" page.
It's the most important weapon in your eBay marketing arsenal!

Allowed on eBay:
DO include a link to your off-eBay website on your "About Me" page.
Encourage visitors to see what other products you have to offer
DO include an opt-in form on your "About Me" page, with a compelling offer.
This could be a newsletter or free report that encourages people to sign up
DO use every possible opportunity in your auction listings and eBay Store.
To encourage people to check out your "About Me" page
Tell them to go to your "About Me" page for information like shipping policies
Tell them to read your FAQ's on your "About Me" page
Tell them to learn more about the products you sell on your "About Me" page
When people buy something, send them **ONE** follow-up email to thank them
Invite them to sign for a newsletter or free report, to get them on an opt-in list.
BUT: They **HAVE** to opt in for you to be able to mail to them!

Create as many reasons as possible to visit your "About Me" page.
Then give them a compelling reason to...
Check out your off-eBay website to see what you offer there

If you do it right, eBay is an excellent client acquisition tool.
You might find it more effective **NOT** to sell your main product on eBay.
Instead sell related products for minimal profit, just to grow your client base.
Then you can back-end sell your main products to them in the future.

Here's an example:
Say you sell an eBook teaching people how to paint water colour flowers.
EBooks are great products in the off-eBay world for you keep 100% of profit.

If you don't count time spent producing them.
But on eBay, eBooks tend to sell relatively cheaply.
So don't sell your eBook there, where you'll take a loss in profit!

Sell something else on eBay.
It should be low cost, low profit and thus low priced.
It should also have some link to your eBook (basic water colour paint set).
Then persuade them to sign up for your opt-in list.
Now you can promote your water colour painting eBook down the road.
You could promote other art-related products too.

EBay regularly changes their policies.
So regularly check so you're following eBay's official seller regulations.
Then you will not experience problems.

WHERE NEXT:

BUT being a professional artist is NOW harder than it ever was.
There are other books that link with this book.
You might need one or more of them:

PRICE RIGHT - Then sell.
http://www.amazon.com/dp/B087S85HS8

PLANNING - Means success.
http://www.amazon.com/dp/B087SCD1NY

CAREER BASICS - Planning.
http://www.amazon.com/dp/B087SCJYX3

FINDING BUYERS - How?
http://www.amazon.com/dp/B087SM58GJ

FIRST WEBSITE - Simple is best.
http://www.amazon.com/dp/B087SFZ6RD

FRAMING = helps sales
http://www.amazon.com/dp/B087SGS6MB

CHRISTMAS - Special approaches.
http://www.amazon.com/dp/B087SHDKPN

TAKE THE PLUNGE - become professional
http://www.amazon.com/dp/B087SFTD61

PRODUCTIVITY – the foundation
http://www.amazon.com/dp/B087S87HLD

COPYRIGHT - making money from copyright sales.
http://www.amazon.com/dp/B0892HWYTV

NOT NOW:

Perhaps one of these books could interest you then?

Write about your own memories.
http://www.amazon.com/dp/B087DWKPTP

A simple way to start developing creativity.
If you are a parent, teacher or someone who meets a group regularly?
http://www.amazon.com/dp/B088T1KFQZ

Here is how most people start becoming an artist!
http://www.amazon.com/dp/B088Y1DPL6

More of my memories.
http://www.amazon.com/dp/B088Y4RPL9

Start an art career but it's **NOW** is harder than it ever was.
http://www.amazon.com/dp/B088T7VJ76

SEND TO:

**Know anyone interested in chocolate recipes?
Then send them this link.**

http://www.amazon.com/dp/B088Y4RPL9

Know anyone interested in THIS book?

http://www.amazon.com/dp/B087SHDKPN

www.ingramcontent.com/pod-product-compliance
Lightning Source LLC
Chambersburg PA
CBHW030950240526
45463CB00016B/2311